DISCARDED
from the Nashville Public Library

THE
FINDHORN
BOOK OF

Meditation

by
Darren John Main

© Darren John Main 2003

First published by Findhorn Press 2003

ISBN 1 84409 005 1

All rights reserved.
The contents of this book may not be reproduced in any form,
except for short extracts for quotation or review,
without the written permission of the publisher.

British Library Cataloguing-in-Publication Data.
A catalogue record for this book is available from
the British Library.

Edited by Tony Mitton
Cover and internal book design by Thierry Bogliolo
Cover background photograph by Digital Vision
Black & white photograph of author on front cover by Jasper Trout

Printed and bound by WS Bookwell, Finland

Published by
Findhorn Press
305a The Park, Findhorn
Forres IV36 3TE
Scotland, UK

tel 01309 690582
fax 01309 690036
e-mail: info@findhornpress.com

findhornpress.com

TABLE OF CONTENTS

*Dedicated to Sue Louiseau
in honor of her tireless editing efforts,
and for always returning to the breath.*

INTRODUCTION

Like most children who were raised in a Western culture, I was not taught meditation as a child. Although I was born into a Roman Catholic family, my personal inquiries into spiritual matters didn't begin until, as a young adult, I chose to look within for my happiness.

It was in 1989 that I began my spiritual path. At the time, I didn't even know what a spiritual path was or where it would lead, but the circumstances of my life had become so uncomfortable that change and death had become my only choices. I was at that proverbial fork in the road.

Although I was only eighteen years old, my body was in sad shape. My muscles hurt, and I often suffered from stomach upsets, abdominal cramps and migraine headaches. Advil and antacids had become staples.

This should not have come as a big surprise since I was living on coffee, fast food and cigarettes. I was also getting by on as little sleep as possible, figuring that I could nap during my high school classes. Although my body appeared to be in good shape inasmuch as I was not overweight, I could not walk up a flight of stairs without losing my breath.

Emotionally and mentally I was in even worse shape. I found myself sunk in frequent bouts of depression that seemed to last for months. Drugs and alcohol were about the only things I could find that would bring me any relief from the dismal pit that my young life had become.

And so by fate, luck or providence, I found myself in an Alcoholics Anonymous meeting – again. It was not my first meeting, but it might as well have been. My desperation and suffering had bottomed in an abyss that forced me to look at the twelve steps with fresh eyes. Although the steps still seemed quite foreign to me, my ever-increasing level of suffering made them seem more and more palatable. They were starting to make sense for the first time. That is, all except for the eleventh step.[1]

Step eleven instructs the alcoholic to create a daily practice of prayer and meditation. In spite of my aversion to the word prayer, that was not my biggest problem with this step. Though tight knots formed in my stomach whenever the word was mentioned, prayer was at least familiar to me.

---

1 Step Eleven: *We sought through prayer and meditation to improve our conscious contact with God as we understand him.*

Meditation was completely alien. Its very mention conjured up images of an old guru with unkempt beard and loincloth on a mountaintop. So I did what any good twelve-stepper would do, I asked my sponsor. Unfortunately, he was not much help. He simply tossed out a few cliché AA slogans like "let go and let God" and "keep it simple." Unsatisfied, I started asking others at meetings but got a similar litany of answers.

And so I sought other venues. I tried self-hypnosis tapes and guided relaxation classes. I went to seminars at new age bookstores and even tried sitting with my eyes closed, waiting for something to happen. I didn't know what I was looking for, but I knew I wasn't finding it.

Fate has a way of putting in your path the things that you most need to find, and I eventually found a meditation group less than five miles from where I was living. It was a small group and was composed entirely of women in their forties. It wasn't what I had envisioned, but I was grateful to have found it.

So every Tuesday night I found myself sitting in a circle chanting "Om" with a bunch of women, any one of whom could have been my mother. There was little that I had in common with the other members of the group, but a deep bond was formed nonetheless.

The glue that held this group together was its facilitator, Ellie. Ellie's gentle manner and compassionate eyes demonstrated to the group what was possible through the practice of meditation. Unlike Ellie's, my life was one drama and upset after another. By contrast, nothing seemed to shock or upset her. It was Ellie who demonstrated that a mindful and centered life was possible and actually gave me the tools and techniques to realize those qualities in myself.

As I began my regular meditation practice, my lifestyle began to change. Within a year, I had quit smoking, cleaned up my diet and started to regulate my sleeping habits. But more than this, my attitude changed. Much of my anger and bitterness toward life began to evaporate, and my relationships became much more civil and better adjusted.

My meditation practice, along with yoga, have now become the centerpiece of my life. They remain as much a part of my daily routine as brushing my teeth.

Several weeks ago, one of my new yoga students stayed after class to ask a few questions. She was about eighteen or nineteen and was looking at me with the same sense of awe as I had once looked at Ellie. Although she was young, it was easy to sense her blossoming commitment to a spiritual life.

"You never seem to be upset," she said. "With all that meditation and yoga, you probably never get angry or upset. It must be nice."

I smiled, because I could hear myself saying those same things to Ellie years before. "I do feel anger and get upset just like everyone. The only difference is that underneath all the ups and downs that life throws my way there is a sense of peace. Emotions like anger and fear still come up. I just don't lose my inner peace quite so easily when they do."

That is what meditation is all about. I have come to believe that learning to quiet the mind and sit in stillness is the greatest gift people can offer themselves.

About This Book

Meditation is quite universal. In one form or another it has been practiced by every culture and religion on earth. It was promoted by the Buddha, Krishna, Jesus, and Mohammed. Countless sages, shamans and healers have been touting this diverse yet universal practice since before the dawn of history.

In fact, our busy modern world is one of the only cultures throughout history that has not placed a noticeable emphasis on spiritual introspection. Sure, many of us attend a church or synagogue – and these activities often bring with them many spiritual benefits – but learning to quiet one's own mind is where we take the lofty principles discussed on Saturdays and Sundays, to make them real and meaningful throughout the week.

In the past, entertainment was something scarce – at least by today's standards. In the nature of things, people had more downtime, and some form of meditation was part of daily life. This is not to say that most people lived like Buddhist monks – they certainly did not – but people did have more quiet time to contemplate who they were and what it was that they wanted out of life.

In our modern world, it is not easy to find some quiet amid the mobile phones and traffic jams, but through the rediscovery of meditation our society can become whole again. And we as individuals can enjoy life more. Really, we have two choices. Either we can learn to quiet the mind and find our contentment and completion within, or we can keep skipping from one thing to the next, hoping that the new car or the new lover will be the answer to our unrest.

In this book I hope to bring back to light some of the wisdom and practices known to our ancestors. We don't need to abandon our modern lives to implement these techniques; we just need to make a little space for them. Meditation can be every bit as useful today as it was in years past. Some would argue that it is needed now more than ever.

This book provides an overview of various aspects of meditation. It is designed to give a basic understanding, both of how to meditate and why meditation is so effective at bringing us a more peaceful experience of life.

I have divided this book into two parts. Part One concerns itself with learning how to meditate. From the basics of finding a seated position that supports your practice to exploring techniques that bring the mind back under control, this section of the book will give you the essential tools needed to get started in your practice.

In Part Two we will explore the mechanics of meditation. It can be very supportive to understand how meditation works and what the process actually looks like. On the surface, meditation can look as if you are sitting around doing nothing. In this section, we will look at the effects of meditation at the psychological, physical and emotional levels. We will also explore the effects of meditation on groups. Because we are all connected at the deepest level of our being, the practice of meditation offers great opportunities for any group of people who practice together – whether that be a husband and wife seeking to deepen their marriage, or the whole human race becoming more peaceful and enlightened as more people find that state of inner balance. Meditation in the context of human relationships is a powerful vehicle for bringing about healing.

It is important to note that meditation is not a religion or a replacement for religion. One can have strong roots in any faith and still benefit from the practice of meditation. In fact, many people find that their own faith deepens as a result of practicing mindfulness. Therefore, you can use these techniques in conjunction with your religion or you can use them as a means to find your own unique relationship with the spiritual.

However you choose to use this book, it is my hope that you will make it personal and unique for you. Meditation is a very individual practice and if you learn to cultivate a practice that is tailored for you and your life, you will find its rewards to be limitless.

This book is a guide to developing one's own meditation practice. It is nothing more than that. There are many wonderful classes and meditation groups out there that will also support you in this inward pursuit, and there are a number of other books that teach a variety of meditation techniques emanating from various cultural and religious points of view. Exploring these other avenues will complement the information contained in this book.

Thirty-One Days

Meditation is a very simple practice. In fact, when people take my 'Introduction to Meditation' workshop, they are often surprised at just how simple the practice is. The most difficult aspect of meditation lies in the commitment to do it daily. This is by far the biggest obstacle to developing a regular and rewarding practice.

It is for this reason that I ask new students to make a one-month commitment to practice daily for at least twenty minutes. This brings several important advantages. First, they gain a month's experience with meditation. During that month, the student has the opportunity to evaluate the practice and begin to feel its many benefits over time. Also, without a regular practice, a student has only my word, or the word of other meditation teachers, to rely on. Blind faith may be enough to get a person started, but it will not be enough to maintain a regular practice.

A month devoted to daily practice will also provide students with the opportunity to form good habits. Meditation should be like any daily habit. Taking care of the mind is every bit as important as taking care of the body. Using this first month to develop good habits will move the practice into the same realm as eating, brushing your teeth and the like. Once the habit is firmly established, taking the time to meditate will become less of a chore and more and more a normal part of your day.

I hope your journey inward will bring you much joy.

May all beings be happy and at peace,

Darren *(www.darrenmain.com)*

Part One

LEARNING HOW TO MEDITATE

Chapter One

LEARNING TO SIT

When I first learned to meditate, I was under the impression that meditation was easy – that it was some kind of relaxation exercise that would leave my body feeling as refreshed as after a gentle nap on a summer afternoon. This was the first in a rather long string of illusions that I held about meditation. It was an illusion that ended with about as much grace as a sparrow flying into a plate glass window.

At my first meditation class with Ellie, I had expected to sit comfortably while my mind drifted off to some magical and quiet place. I was excited about leaving my rather uncomfortable body behind for a bit, and I could feel a soft bounce in my step as I walked up the sidewalk to her yoga studio. *Learning to meditate was going to be just what I needed to overcome the discomfort that was my life.*

After some brief introductions and a short overview on how to meditate, we sat in a circle, around some candles in the center, and began the practice. All went well for the first minute or two. It wasn't what I expected of course. There were no bolts of lightning and the voice of God didn't come booming down from the clouds. Nevertheless, I was sitting quietly.

Then I felt something very unexpected. My foot began to fall asleep. "Not a problem," I thought. "It will pass." No such luck. The pins and needles didn't stop. In fact, they got worse. They traveled up my legs until I cracked open my eyes to see if my feet had turned blue. Thankfully they had not. But while my eyes were open, I took a glance around the room. Everyone looked like a stone statue of the Buddha – still, quiet and anchored in peace.

I closed my eyes again and felt the numbness begin to subside. "Now I will get to the good stuff!" I thought. But the numbness only gave way to aching hips, a sore back and knees that felt as if there were shards of glass inside them. On top of all that, my head hurt from trying to ignore the agony of my body. I was just about to get up and walk out of the room when I heard Ellie's voice coaxing us out of meditation.

After the meditation, each person had a chance to share. All of them seemed to have had a positive experience. One woman even cried a bit because she had found such a peaceful state. I could understand wanting to cry too, but peace was the furthest thing from my mind! Even though I had shifted positions, I still felt as if someone had taken a razor strap to my low back.

When it was my turn to share, I didn't know what to do. I had obviously done something wrong. Both my mind and my body were in complete hell. I decided to be honest rather than pretend. After all, I didn't plan on coming back, so I had no reason to lie. "Well, first off, I don't know what you folks did to make your meditation so wonderful, but I hated it. My body has never felt worse, and my mind feels like an animal chasing its own tail. Either I did something really wrong, or you are all masochists."

Ellie smiled and quietly let me finish my tirade before she responded. "Darren, meditation is not an easy practice, and sitting still is not easy for most of us. In the West, we are not encouraged to sit and go within for our answers. In fact, we are not encouraged to sit still at all. Our minds will resist this process – especially in the beginning stages of our practice. But if you are patient, you will work through many of these seemingly insurmountable obstacles."

There was something about her calmness that reassured me. She also showed me some ways to sit that would be less challenging to my body. I decided to give it another shot, and came back the following week. That was the start of a new relationship with my body and my mind. Sitting can be difficult at times, even after years of meditation, but in general it has become much easier over the years.

In this first chapter, I would like to address some of the physical issues that come up when we meditate. The good news is that many of the techniques and suggestions I offer in this chapter will help alleviate much of the discomfort that I experienced during that first meditation. However, one point needs to be stressed. Although there are many things you can do to make yourself more comfortable, a certain amount of discomfort is to be expected. In fact, that discomfort is part of the practice. Know that as your practice progresses, sitting will become easier. The key to success is not to give up.

How to Sit

For seated meditation, there is only one rule that needs to be observed. Everything else is merely a suggestion that you can use or dismiss as you see fit. The essential rule is, quite simply, to keep the spine straight. Slouching, lounging, lying down and leaning are all the kiss of death to a strong meditation practice. Therefore, learning to sit in a comfortable upright position is paramount to a rewarding and long-term practice.

Try this little experiment. Sit in a nice tall upright position. Feel your spine lengthen and lift your chest a bit. Notice how that feels. Your mind and your body are very connected, so it is fundamental to put your body in a position that says "attention." Now try slouching. Round your shoulders forward and let your head hang. A position such as this is likely to evoke drowsiness and invite your mind to wander. Lying down, while perfect for relaxation and sleep, will make the practice of meditation very difficult.

Reminder
> Meditation is a time to focus, train the mind and bring it to stillness. It is not a time to rest and relax.

Because it is so important to sit upright, there are several preferred positions. As far as meditation is concerned, all of them work equally well, so try to find the position that works best for you. Learning to sit on the floor rather than on a chair has its advantages, but don't feel that it is a requirement.

The Lotus Pose

About a year ago, I was teaching a meditation class to a group of fifth graders. They were very excited to be learning just about anything other than math and English. I started the class the way I start many of my meditation workshops – by asking the group what they knew about meditation.

Immediately a bunch of hands went up and I called on an enthusiastic boy in the front row who looked as if he was going to jump out of his skin, he was so sure of himself. No sooner did I call on him than he hopped out of his seat, sat on the floor and wrapped one leg over the other. He then closed his eyes and started making the sound of 'om.' Naturally all the students laughed and started 'Om-ing' right along with him.

What he was doing was not meditation itself, but a popular sitting pose called lotus. This pose is perfect for sitting as it tips the pelvis slightly forward, which encourages the spine to be straight and tall. This gives greater support to the spine and back, and one can sit longer with less discomfort.

Unfortunately there is a little catch. If you have tight knees or hips, it will be extremely painful, if not impossible, to sit in lotus. This is where hatha yoga really supports a practice. By working to keep the hips and legs open, hatha yoga makes the lotus posture much more accessible. To learn this pose, I recommend consulting an experienced hatha yoga teacher in order to avoid injury.

Half Lotus Pose

Because most of us don't start a meditation practice until adulthood, there is a good chance that our hips and knees will be too tight for the lotus. Therefore, most people need to use a meditation cushion and a modified pose called the half lotus.

In the half lotus pose, your legs stack one on top of the other. This provides some of the same benefits as the full lotus, but allows you to open your hips rather more slowly. The effects are not quite as dramatic, but it is a much more realistic alternative for most people living in Western cultures.

Because the half lotus is modified, most people need additional support. This is where a meditation cushion is helpful. The cushion should not be too soft – in fact, the firmer the better. There are a number of stores and yoga studios that sell cushions designed for sitting. (See Appendix C.) You can also use a firm, folded blanket.

Proper placement of the cushion or blanket is very important. Rather than sit on it with the back of the legs as you would sit on a chair, you will want to sit so that your buttocks are on the cushion and your legs are on the floor. This will help to tilt the pelvis forward and will encourage that straight spine.

Tip	Take some hatha yoga classes. The practice of hatha yoga was designed to help people sit in meditation for long periods of time. In addition to its many physical benefits, hatha yoga is sure to make your meditation practice a lot more comfortable.

Chairs and Benches

Sitting on the floor with legs crossed can be a very grounding experience and can be a wonderful part of your practice. However, if you spend your whole time in agony, you will have a very short meditation career. For some people, sitting with crossed legs is simply not an option, and other means are suggested.

One option is a meditation bench. These benches are designed to take most pressure off the knees while encouraging the spine to remain straight. They can be easily built or ordered from a number of companies. (See Appendix C.)

Sitting on these benches is simple enough. From a kneeling position, place the bench behind you, above your calves. Now sit back, placing your buttocks on the bench. I find it helpful to put some padding under the knees as well. A blanket folded several times works quite well.

For some people, especially senior citizens, getting on the floor is not an option. In these cases I suggest using a straight-backed chair. This allows for a straight spine and an alert mind without the problem of getting up and down. The important detail here lies in the choice of chairs. Something like a couch or lazy boy would not be very supportive. Although these types of chairs are well suited for watching TV or taking a nap, they tend to keep the mind in a less than focused state. It's best to choose a chair that is firm and has a straight back. Also, try to choose something that will allow the feet to be planted firmly on the floor.

Time

When learning to sit in meditation, we also need to think about timing. There are two basic questions that need answering before we can proceed. The first one is, how long will I meditate today? And the second, when will I meditate?

Regular meditation is much more important than sporadic sits, even if those sits are longer. In other words, you will experience more benefit from sitting for fifteen minutes every day than from sitting for one hour once or twice a week.

Therefore it is important to decide when you will meditate and for how long. For myself, I prefer meditating first thing in the morning. This has two benefits. First, it starts my day off on the right foot. This doesn't guarantee a great day, but I have found there is a definite correlation between the days that I start with meditation and the days that seem to run more smoothly. I have also found that meditating first thing insures that I make the time to sit. I am much more likely to forget to meditate if I try to make time for it later in my day.

Of course not everyone is a morning person. Some people prefer to meditate on their lunch break or just before dinner. One thing that most people find helpful, however, is to make it part of a regular routine. One way to do this is to meditate at the same time each day.

When Not to Meditate
- After a large meal
- Just before bed
- After drinking caffeine

Good times to Meditate
- First thing in the morning
- Before meals
- Several hours before bed

The other thing to consider about timing is how long you will choose to sit. I would recommend sitting for at least fifteen minutes. Short meditations of ten minutes or less are not without benefits, but to really start getting into the deeper realms of the mind, a minimum of fifteen minutes is necessary.

Of course, it is preferable to sit for longer than fifteen minutes. In fact, I encourage my new meditation students to sit for twenty minutes, and my more advanced students to sit for thirty minutes or more. Meditation is a lot like cardiovascular exercise where you need to do a minimum amount of time to shift the body into aerobic mode, and every minute past the minimum is burning more calories. The mind works the same way. Every minute you spend in meditation after that initial fifteen minutes is taking you deeper and deeper into the unconscious mind.

The important thing is that you choose an amount of time that you can commit to. Deciding to meditate for forty-five minutes each day is great, but if you only pay lip service to it, you are not doing yourself any favors. You will benefit more by choosing a shorter period of time, such as twenty minutes, and doing it consistently than by having lofty intentions and never actualizing those ideals in your life.

Tip To time yourself, take a small clock or watch and place it on the floor in front of you. Before you close your eyes to meditate, look at the time and figure out the time when your meditation will be over, e.g., when the big hand is on the four and the time is twenty past. This saves you from having to do math while you are trying to meditate.

Once you start your meditation, you can peek from time to time to see how much longer you have. After a while, you will have to peek less and less, but in the beginning this can be a helpful way to make sure your meditations start and end on time. Another option is to find a timer with a very gentle bell. You don't want to be jolted out of your meditation.

Although we have covered a lot of information about how to sit, we have still not discussed the actual practice of meditation. Everything we have covered in this chapter will be a foundation for what is to come in the rest of the book.

Chapter Two

TRAINING THE MIND

On one of my annual retreats to Costa Rica a few years back, I decided to offer the students a basic meditation workshop. Whenever I lead this workshop, I like to survey the group to see how much they know about meditation and what misconceptions they may have about the practice. It is also helpful to know what people hope to get from the workshop.

One man had this to say in response to my inquiry. "Being on this retreat has been great. I feel better than I have felt in a long time. The one thing I haven't been able to do is get my mind to shut off completely. I am hoping that you will give me a meditation technique that will allow me to turn off my mind whenever I want to."

The other students nodded and smiled in agreement. I had to chuckle to myself because I knew exactly where he was coming from. When I first started meditating, I was looking for the right technique or a sacred mantra to undo the years of craziness that existed in my mind. I knew there had to be a technique out there that would work for me – something that would end the madness of my mind once and for all.

Unfortunately for me, for the people on that retreat and for anyone who has ever tried meditation, there is no magic pill. There is no one technique that is easy and foolproof, and there is no fairy godmother who will tap you on the head with the wand of enlightenment. The realization that meditation is work – lots of work – is the first thing that we need to address before we can look at the practice itself.

Think about it. You have probably spent your whole life believing that thoughts are just something that happen to you. If you are like most people, you have been feeling like a victim of those thoughts when they make you unhappy and like royalty when they make you feel good.

The mind and all its thoughts seem to be happening by accident because we have let the mind get out of shape and become undisciplined. We have countless ways to entertain the mind and distract it from boredom. We have any number of ways to justify our thoughts and the emotions and actions that inevitably follow those thoughts. And we have become masters of projection – pushing the responsibility for our own thoughts outward so that the consequences of our thoughts become someone else's problem.

All this we have done for years. Our untrained minds have deep habitual grooves carved into them – grooves that desperately need to be sanded down and retrained through the practice of meditation. However, doing this is not going to be easy. These mental habits and patterns are sure to trip us up and distract us over and over again as we practice.

Tip   No matter how many times you get distracted during your meditation, RETURN to the practice. Everyone gets distracted all the time. It is the nature of the ego mind to get distracted. The practice of meditation involves realizing you have become distracted and then returning to the practice without judgment. It serves no purpose to beat yourself up for becoming distracted.

Now in the case of the man who attended the meditation workshop in Costa Rica, I had to break the bad news to him. He was disappointed that I wasn't going to offer him an easy way out of his busy mind, and so were many of the other students in the class, but there was a positive side. While meditation is not an easy out, it is a very effective way to train the mind. Although it is a lot of work, it is a lot less work than letting the mind run amok. The good news is that the mind can be trained and brought under control.

The other day I was sitting in the park with my laptop, writing the introduction to this book. There was a woman walking her dog, or I should rather say, the dog was walking her. She was a small woman, and her dog was rather large. The leash was pulled tight and her time was spent screaming obscenities at the dog and trying to manage its unruly desire to chase other dogs, bark at strangers and mark every tree it could find.

The scene was quite funny, but what really completed the picture was another woman who came walking up behind her. She also had a dog, but her dog followed her. It was not on a leash and didn't need to be. This woman spent her time playing with her pet. She threw a tennis ball and wrestled with her dog in the grass.

This is the choice we make when we start meditation. We are choosing to train the mind. Rather than letting the mind drag us through life on a leash, the mind becomes our friend and companion. Just as a puppy can be trained to follow you and sit when you tell it, the mind can also be trained. But discipline and commitment are needed. Dogs don't magically become well behaved, and neither do minds. Just as training a puppy takes practice and can be a lot of work, so training the mind is not always easy and the commitment to the training process is long-term. However, the benefits of taking control of the mind will affect every aspect of life.

Types of Meditation

Whenever I say that I teach meditation, everyone seems to ask, "What kind of meditation do you teach?" This is an understandable question because there are hundreds or thousands of different meditation techniques. Some of them are connected to religious traditions while others are more neutral.

In general, all meditation techniques fall into one of four categories. Understanding these basic categories will help you ultimately pick a style of meditation that is best suited for you. Let's look at each of these categories in turn.

Mantra Meditations

The word mantra means 'sacred sound' or 'sacred word' in the Sanskrit language. Although the word mantra comes from the East, it describes any number of techniques from all over the world. Mantra meditation is the repetition of a word, phrase or prayer. This helps to keep the mind focused and opens a person up to deeper states of awareness. This mantra can be in an ancient language like Hebrew, Latin or Sanskrit or it can be a more modern word such as love or peace. A few examples of mantra meditation include Transcendental Meditation, the Hindu practice of Japa, and the Christian Rosary.

Contemplative Meditations

A great way to train the mind is to keep it focused on a concept or idea. In our world of bright and sexy images, it is not easy to focus on the deeper meaning of a riddle or scriptural passage, but that is what the contemplative traditions ask of their students. Generally speaking, a student of this style of meditation chooses (or is given) a concept on which to reflect. This can be anything from a paradoxical question to a passage from a religious text. Examples of contemplative meditation include Zen koans, Jana yoga, and centering prayer.

Visualization Meditations

One way to keep the mind focused is to hold an image in the mind's eye. For people who tend to be more visual, this can be a very useful technique. Some people will envision something simple, such as a candle flame or a religious symbol. Other people will visualize the image of a saint, guru or deity. Visualization meditations should not be confused with hypnosis or guided visualizations. There is a distinct and well-defined difference. Visualization meditation is about focusing the mind on a single and relatively unchanging image. Guided visualizations and hypnosis generally keep the mind very active and often involve an ever-changing narration. This is not to say that the guided experience is not helpful. Indeed, for many people it can be profoundly helpful. However, it is not a substitute for a regular meditation practice.

Body-centered Meditations

The nice thing about the body is that it is always in the present moment. This means that bringing the focus to the body is a quick and effective way to focus the mind. Also, body-centered meditations are usually neutral in respect of religious beliefs, so they are a bit easier to integrate into your own individual beliefs. Some styles of body-centered meditation focus on the breath while others focus on sensation in the body. Some even focus on movement. Styles of body-centered meditation include hatha yoga, Tai Chi and Vipassana meditation.

A Technique to Get You Started

As I have mentioned, there are countless styles of meditation. I would like to teach you my personal favorite, which you can use to get started. You may find that this technique is perfectly suited to you and you may choose to use it for years to come, or you may find another technique that works better for you. If that is the case, I encourage you to use that technique instead.

The Buddha was once asked which meditation technique was the most effective. The master's response was both simple and profound: "The one you practice." Therefore, start your practice with this simple technique and explore others as well. The important thing is that you get started and that you practice consistently.

Sit in a comfortable upright position. Some people sit cross-legged, others prefer to kneel. It is also acceptable to sit in a straight-backed chair (see Chapter One.) Allow your body to relax and take a few deep, full breaths to shift into a quiet space.

As you begin to quiet down, focus on the sensation of the breath as it flows in and out of the nose where it touches the upper lip. There is no need to change the quality of the breath. Simply watch it move in and out. You will find that the mind will frequently wander. This is natural. Once you notice that the mind has wandered, gently bring it back to the breath.

The whole process is one of bringing the mind back to the breath over and over again. Try not to be discouraged by how much the mind will wander. You have been letting your mind wander undisciplined for many years. You can't expect it to sit still overnight. Rather than chastising yourself for letting your mind wander, praise yourself for noticing, and gently bring it back.

Practice Session

>Before moving on to the next chapter, I recommend that you sit and meditate for at least twenty minutes and start to develop a daily practice. This will give you a point of reference as we look in more detail at the whole subject of meditation.

Chapter Three

The Obstacles to Stillness

In the last chapter we looked at some of the basic types of meditation that are available and learned a simple technique for getting started. Now we are going to refine our skills even further. If you have started your meditation practice as suggested at the end of chapter two, you have no doubt realized that it is much more difficult than you might have expected. In this chapter, we are going to look at the very things that make the practice difficult and provide you with some practical tips for dealing with these distractions.

When I first began my meditation practice, I thought I was crazy. I would sit to meditate, and my mind wouldn't be still. All I had to do was one simple thing. Watch the breath. But my mind would twist and turn like a cat trying to avoid a bath. I wondered what was wrong with me. I thought for sure that I was completely insane and that no one else could possibly be as disturbed as I was.

What I have learned through my years of practice, and even more through my teaching, is that I am by no means unique. Everyone struggles with meditation. Everyone feels as if they are ready for an insane asylum. The games that the mind plays to keep us distracted are not unique either. One would think that, with the vast capacity of the human brain, there would be thousands of ways to keep us distracted when in fact there are only five. Once we learn these five 'mind games', we can begin to see through them and take back control of the mind.

Before we learn to handle these five obstacles, however, it is helpful to understand a few things about the mind itself. We are going to be covering the psychology of the mind in a later chapter, but for now we will be content to ask the question, "Who am I?"

Practice Session

Sit with your eyes closed for a minute or two and consider the question, "Who am I?" Feel free to make a list in your head of the things that define you. Statements like, "I am a mother," or, "I am an accountant," are likely to fill your head. Most of your answers, however, will not be WHO you are. These false beliefs about yourself are part of a spiritual identity crisis called 'the ego'.

As human beings, we have two identities. One is real, and the other is an illusion. As odd as this may sound, it is quite true. In writing, the real Self is usually depicted with a capital 'S'; it is the part of the mind that exists in a natural state of peace. It exists in a constant state of knowing and doesn't become upset and turbulent. This is the part of the mind with which we are seeking to get more connected through the practice of meditation.

This true Self is not identified by the details of one's life. Things like jobs, relationships and recreation can be expressions of this true Self, but are never confused with it. The Self stands on its own and is complete without external or finite labels.

The false self is commonly referred to as 'the ego' and could not be more different. The ego defines itself by its judgments and stories. It believes it *is* the experiences it has had in life *and* the judgments it holds about those experiences. Its core belief is that it is separate and small. It feels, and rightly so, that if it lets its guard down for even a second, the vastness of the true Self would eclipse it. Therefore, the ego has a vested interest in keeping the mind busy. When we sit still in meditation, we begin to quiet the ego mind and start to listen to the true Self. To our egos, this is the most dangerous thing we can do.

In light of this, we can easily see why the ego struggles to keep the mind busy. When we sit still, the ego is not happy. In fact it is downright upset. That is why it has devised the five obstacles mentioned earlier. These five obstacles are very clever tricks, but with a little mindfulness they can be understood. Our ego uses these tricks when we are living our day-to-day lives, but they don't really become evident until we try to quiet the mind.

Reminder

> The ego mind exists because of the constant churnings of thought that it creates. If you are struggling to quiet the mind during meditation, you can be sure it is because the ego senses you are close to realizing

something important. That's when the ego decides to kick up some dust. The best thing you can do in these situations is stay committed to your practice.

Craving

In the West, we live in great material abundance. Pleasures to stimulate every sense abound at every corner. We have movies filled with special effects to give us eye candy, and stereos to massage our ears. Food has become much more about flavor, and its function to support and nourish the body is often overlooked. While there is nothing innately wrong with enjoying the pleasurable aspects of life, it can become burdensome – especially when you are trying to meditate.

It is important to note that there are natural instincts such as our appetite and our sex drive that guide us and help preserve our health and survival. These 'appetites' are normal and natural; however, the ego will warp those impulses and use them for its own goals. Some examples of the ego's warped impulses are overeating, acting out sexually, and any number of other destructive behaviors.

As we live our lives, it is important to learn to distinguish between an ego craving and a natural body appetite. If we get confused between the two, as many of us often do, trouble is sure to follow. In normal life it is not always easy, learning to distinguish between a craving and an appetite. But in meditation practice you can be sure that what you're feeling is almost always craving.

If you were to sit for twenty or thirty minutes or even an hour, it is unlikely that you would have any real biological needs except for oxygen. Food, water, sex and the other natural body appetites can safely be put on hold for much more than an hour. Therefore, it is almost always inappropriate to give in to a craving when you are meditating.

Our ego mind loves pleasurable things. It seeks them out all day long, and when we close our eyes to meditate those cravings don't stop. In fact, those cravings can intensify because we are not catering to them.

When we sit and meditate, cravings are one of the key ways that the ego mind uses to keep us distracted. Because, for most of us, it is such a pattern in our lives to satisfy our cravings, the ego simply extends this pattern into our meditation practice. For me in the beginning, it was one of the most effective ways the ego had of pulling me away from my breath.

This morning when I sat to meditate, I could feel my mind spinning out of control with cravings. First, I wanted to see what was on the news. I was sure something major was happening. More than anything I wanted to get up and turn on one of those cable news stations. I resisted that craving, however, and did my best to return to my breath. Then I had a thought. What if I am right? I could prove that meditation has made me more psychic if I just get up and turn on the TV. After all, it would be done in the name of my practice. I continued with this line of thinking for almost five minutes and I almost convinced myself to end my practice early, just so I could satisfy my craving for the news.

My experience this morning is not unlike the ones you will probably have as you practice. Of course you may not have a craving for news. It may be for a snack or some other sensual pleasure. It may not even be something that involves getting up. It may be enough for your ego to keep you in a dialog about the thing you are craving. Cravings can be very strong. In fact, many people find them overwhelming. That is why it is so important not to give in to them.

It is also very important to learn to deal with them. A meditation practice doesn't require us to suffer. But it does ask us to resist temptation. The ego would love nothing more than to have us run to the refrigerator or turn on the news. It knows that once we do, the meditation is over and it gets to keep its job.

Therefore, in the context of your meditation practice, the only way to deal with craving is not to give in to it. As I mentioned above, the only thing we really need for the length of our practice is oxygen. Everything else can wait. Once you give in to that craving, the ego will know what works. It's like trying to teach a dog not to beg and then feeding it scraps of food under the table. You are teaching your ego that cravings will distract you and, knowing what an effective tool they are, it will use cravings all the time.

It is usually pretty difficult to resist cravings. But there are a few concrete things you can do to help address the cravings as they come up.

1. *Acknowledge the craving.* If you are craving food simply say, "Craving food." Look at it for what it is. Once you realize that it is an ego game, it will become that much easier to return to the breath. The cravings may go away once you acknowledge them, or they may not. But whatever happens, you will be better prepared to stop yourself acting on them.

2. *Avoid moving into fantasy.* We will discuss fantasy later in this chapter as it is one of the other obstacles, but it can work hand in hand with craving. If you are craving a piece of chocolate cake, letting the mind run wild with a fantasy about how great it will taste

is only going to make matters worse. If you find yourself going down that road, be sure to acknowledge what you are doing and return to the breath.

3. *Give yourself permission.* Assuming you are craving something that will not hurt you, give yourself permission to work through the craving after your meditation. When I was wanting to see what was happening in the world, I gave myself permission to turn on the TV after my practice. This was very helpful in letting me return to the breath. Interestingly, I no longer wanted to turn on the news when I had finished. This often happens with cravings that come up during a practice.

4. *Don't get up until your time is up.* If you cut your meditation short because of your cravings, the ego has won. You may not be able to spend much time with the breath and you may be very uncomfortable, but if you get up and cater to the ego's cravings, it will only make your next meditation more difficult.

Tip   Cravings will come up during your meditation prac-
        tice. There is nothing wrong with experiencing crav-
        ings. The important thing is not to give in to them. If
        you do, you will only invite more.

Aversion

Just as the ego would have you spend a lot of time looking for pleasure and has a short list of cravings that it loves to engage in, so it also has a strong desire to avoid the uncomfortable. This ego practice is called aversion. Like its cousin craving, aversion shows up in life and acts even more vigorously when we come to the meditation cushion.

Backing away from pain is not necessarily a bad thing. It is a very natural part of our survival instinct. For example, if you were to stick your big toe into a tub full of hot water, you would naturally pull your foot back to protect yourself. If you didn't have this basic instinct, you would jump into the water and your whole body would be scalded.

Just as the ego takes the body's natural appetites and exploits them to create cravings, so it creates aversions by exploiting our natural resistance to physical pain. An aversion is based on the same principle as resistance to pain, but it is not real. In fact, it can oftentimes cause more pain than was actually avoided.

My parents were married for twenty-five years. They had some good times of course, but much of their marriage was strained, to say the least. Both of them knew it wasn't working. Neither spoke to the other about it, nor ever showed any verbal or physical affection. In addition, neither seemed to want to work on improving the marriage.

Divorce is a difficult process. I don't know anyone who has enjoyed the experience. It is certainly not something one would look forward to, but it is, at times, necessary. This was the case with my parents.

They lived with each other in a constant state of suffering, but neither wanted to walk though the uncomfortable process of divorce. This is a classic example of aversion.

After twenty-five years together, my mother finally asked my father for a divorce. It was not easy for either of them. Letting go of the past and wondering about the future during mid-life must have been very challenging, but in this case it was for the best. When the ego uses aversion, it convinces us that because something is difficult or uncomfortable, it must be dangerous and should be avoided.

I had a similar experience when I gave up smoking. Quitting smoking is one of the most difficult and uncomfortable things a person can do. Of course, not quitting will ultimately make for an even more uncomfortable situation. The ego, however, doesn't look at the big picture. That is why it took me several years of trying before I was actually able to quit. The ego had me focused on the discomfort of the moment rather than the bigger picture.

When we sit and meditate, the ego will use the full force of this aversion principle. The ego loves to create stories about why it is better to get up and do something else, rather than meditate. If it can't convince you to stop the meditation altogether, then it will settle for busying the mind with all sorts of entertaining stories. In either case, when you find yourself in aversion mode, you are very likely close to a breakthrough. Just as was true of craving, the key is not to give in, in this case to the desire to avoid. Here are a few things you can do that may help you resist aversion:

1. ***Acknowledge that you are in aversion.*** This may sound odd, but sometimes just acknowledging it can bring you back to the breath.

2. ***Remind yourself that you are safe.*** When you are sitting in meditation, there is no waiting tub of scalding water and nothing to be afraid of. Therefore, whatever is coming up is a game that the ego is playing.

3. ***Don't give in to the aversion.*** If you do, the ego will use it all the time.

Dealing with aversion is not easy. The things that come up can seem very real and can be very uncomfortable. But like giving up cigarettes, the benefit of not catering to the aversion is well worth the effort. On the other side of that discomfort is liberation from the ego's bondage.

Agitation

Back when I was trying to quit smoking, aversion was not the only thing that came up. Agitation was right there too. I call this the pacing tiger syndrome. It is something like aversion in that it feels very uncomfortable, but it carries a more general sense of discomfort, one that you can't put your finger on. You don't know what you want. Whereas aversion and craving are associated with a definite need or desire, agitation is not. In many ways this makes it more difficult to address.

Agitation is not something you can pinpoint. It is a feeling of dis-ease, a discomfort with the current situation but with no solution at hand. It is like standing with a growling stomach in front of the refrigerator door and not knowing what you want to eat. The ego loves agitation because it generally results in a person hopping around like a madman who has just stubbed his toe.

When we are on the meditation cushion, agitation is bound to come up. For me personally, it is my ego's favorite game. There is no one thing that I want to do. I just don't want to be where I am. I also find myself fidgeting a lot. For me, agitation often comes with the sensation of a tickle or scratch someplace on my body. Of course, as soon as I break down and scratch it, my ego creates another and another until I am in a virtual seizure, scratching myself and adjusting my position.

Dealing with agitation is not going to be easy, and I wish I could say that I have a simple and easy way to get around it. Unfortunately, I can't. What I do have are a few pieces of advice on how to address agitation when it comes up.

1. Acknowledge the agitation, and if its origin is apparent, you can acknowledge that as well. Like the previous two obstacles, you can often make agitation drift away by simply shining the light of awareness on it.

2. Make subtle adjustments to your posture, but be very mindful not to let the ego take you for a ride. Sometimes it is better to sit with a modest amount of physical discomfort than to let the ego lead you through a gymnastic routine during your meditation.

3. Don't cater to your agitation. If you give your ego its way and get up before the appointed time, you will find that agitation will visit most of your meditations and you will never be free. If you can stick it out, you will find that agitation will be your companion less and less often.

It is not going to be easy to get around agitation. That can't be stressed enough, but like the other obstacles to one's peace of mind, it creates even more difficulties if you don't deal with it as it comes up. Remember that what we experience during our meditation practice is a model of how we interact with life. If we can learn to face our agitations on the meditation cushion, we will find that our reactions to life itself will become more centered and peaceful.

Fantasy

The other day I found myself half asleep in the shower, thinking about a run-in I had had with one of the guests at a book signing. I was in a small town in the central valley of California, and a few conservative 'Christians' had decided it was their job to come to my talk about yoga and inform me that I was teaching 'the devil's dance'. They were friendly enough with their assertions, but their comments were certainly out of line.

Ever since my first book came out and I started putting myself in the public eye, I have encountered people like this – folks who disagree with me and feel the need to tell me so while I am standing in front of a crowd with a microphone in hand. I have learned to acknowledge them and their opinions and then move back to my own talk. This usually pacifies them.

In this case, the people in question were very upset because a friend of theirs had found yoga and rarely went to church with them anymore. This of course fueled their 'devil's dance' perception. Although our interactions were brief, I found that I was left with a feeling of incompletion because they had walked out while I was in mid-sentence.

So when I found myself in the shower, half asleep, it was all too easy to drift into fantasy mode. I would rehash the scenario over and over, changing details and thinking about the things I could have said or done differently. In some of the fantasies they stuck around and decided to take up yoga. In others they left, but I had a very clever quip as they walked out the door.

Of course none of it mattered because it was not what had actually happened. It wasn't until the shower started to run cold and I had to rinse the conditioner out of my hair, polar bear style, that I was able to break free from my ego's fantasy world.

Fantasy is something that we do all the time, but mostly on an unconscious level. The ego is a master storyteller and it loves to hear itself speak. Its stories have nothing to do with reality. In fact they have everything to do with preventing a person from seeing reality.

These fantasies can be nice or they can be ugly. They can be somewhat realistic or they can be completely far-fetched. From a meditation point of view it doesn't really matter. The ego uses fantasy to keep the mind busy in unreality. Rather than be in the present moment, which is the only place where reality can be experienced, the ego would have us living in the future or the past.

Of course, we can clearly see how this is played out in real life. You can fantasize about becoming a writer or an actor or making a difference in the world. But all the fantasies ever dreamed up have not been enough to make that become a reality. Sculpting the future and healing the past can only happen through action in the present moment.

When we meditate we seek to ground the mind in the present moment. We focus on the breath or the image of a saint or a mantra. All of this is designed to keep the mind present, so we can choose to let go of past baggage and our attachments to what the future should hold. The ego doesn't like this, so it uses fantasy to lure the mind out of the present moment.

I have found that when I will not give in to craving, aversion and agitation, the ego smiles and says "Okay, you won't end this meditation, so I will keep your mind busy until it is over. Have fun . . ." Make no mistake about it. Avoiding fantasy is not easy. Even when you realize it is a fantasy the temptation to engage in it remains powerful. Choosing to disengage from a fantasy can be extremely difficult. Here are some suggestions on how to deal with fantasy when it comes up.

1. When you realize you are in the midst of a fantasy, don't waste time judging it. Some fantasies will be pleasant; others would land you in jail if you acted them out. Whatever the fantasy, acknowledge that it is not real and return to the breath.

2. Many fantasies have a very strong pull. Even if you manage to return to the breath once, you may find yourself back in the middle of the fantasy over and over again. Try not to judge yourself for this. Instead, simply return to the breath over and over again.

3. Try to avoid media (TV, news, and Internet) just before meditating. Its only effect will be to provide the ego with fantasy material. There is nothing more enjoyable than arguing religion and politics when you don't have a real opponent to argue back.

4. Always remember that your fantasies are not real and don't deserve your attention.

Sloth

The last trick the ego uses to distract us, both in life and meditation practice, is sloth. Sloth can take many forms: sometimes, emotional depression; at others, mental 'dopiness'; at still others, physical fatigue.

Sometimes these feelings have legitimate biological causes. For instance, some forms of depression are organic (caused by a chemical imbalance in the brain); and a person will certainly be physically tired at the end of a long day of heavy labor. However, many times sloth has nothing to do with legitimate circumstances and is, in fact, manufactured by the ego.

Have you ever spent a day doing nothing and found at the end that you were more tired than on days when you were highly productive? This is the ego at work. Sloth is not about physical, emotional, or mental fatigue. Sloth is about the ego telling the mind to go to sleep. Learning to spot the difference between sloth and genuine fatigue is key. Both natural fatigue and depression, as well as the sloth that is manufactured by the ego, can interfere with meditation practice. However, each must be dealt with in different ways.

Let's look at the non-ego-based fatigue first. As we mentioned, this can manifest itself on all three levels: mental, emotional and physical. Our best way of dealing with this natural form of fatigue is through lifestyle changes and there are a number of things we can do. Here are a few:

- Have a regular time to wake up.

- Have a regular bedtime.

- Avoid caffeine (even in the morning).

- Sleep six to eight hours EVERY night.

- Avoid oversleeping (too much sleep is just as bad as not enough).

- Don't meditate just before bed.

- Give yourself enough time to wake up before a morning meditation.

- Don't lie down to meditate.

For organic depression and mental lethargy the following tips may help:

- Avoid refined sugars.

- Be sure to exercise regularly.

- Get the right amount of sleep each night.

- Avoid meat and foods high in fats.

- See an herbalist for suggested herbs.

- If none of the above helps, see a doctor.

While these lifestyle suggestions are sure to make your time sitting on the cushion easier, they are not directly connected to meditation. However, observing some or all of the above suggestions will make the identification and management of ego-based sloth much easier. It is difficult enough to deal with ego-based sloth by itself. If you are feeling depressed or are overtired, it will be a real uphill battle.

When my ego uses sloth to distract me from my meditation, I sometimes find my mind wandering into a dreamlike state. Soon I find my head nodding and my posture slumping. This ego game is especially difficult because you are half-asleep for the whole thing. Needless to say, your mind is far from your breath, and you would much rather go to bed than sit in meditation.

In dealing with sloth on the meditation cushion, the first step is to choose times to meditate when you will not be tired before you start. For example, after a heavy meal or just before bed are not the best times. Choose times when you are not likely to want a nap. Before meals tends to be best for most people.

Second, if you find yourself getting drowsy, try shifting positions and deepening the breath a bit. This can snap you out of it and help bring a bit more oxygen to the brain. Many times, I find this enough to make me more alert and bring my focus back to the breath.

If all else fails, you can stand up to meditate. The eyes will remain closed and the focus will remain on the breath, but the body will need to keep the mind more alert to prevent you falling over. Eventually, you can sit back down. The ego usually tires of standing and will stop trying to put you to sleep when you return to a seated position. Here are a few additional tips:

- Finish your meditation – even if you feel like you are not getting anywhere.

- NEVER lie down to meditate.

- Don't use drugs such as caffeine to keep you awake or you will find yourself dealing with the agitation obstacle.

- Wash your hands and face before meditation. This can make you feel more refreshed and prepared to sit.

The above obstacles are not easy to overcome, but the suggestions I have listed will make it simpler. The key is awareness. Once we recognize the ego's games, they become that much easier to avoid. The first time you walk down the path you may trip over a stump, but once you know it is there, you will be less likely to fall. You may trip from time to time when you are not paying attention, but acknowledging the pitfalls will go a long way toward avoiding them.

The next step in learning to meditate is learning to identify these obstacles as they appear and continuing to return to the breath in spite of them. By acknowledging these distractions we train the mind to become more vigilant toward them, and as we do this we trip over them less and less. This is a great benefit in one's meditation practice and an even bigger benefit in life.

Practice Session

From now on when you meditate, try to identify the obstacle that distracts you. As you find your mind somewhere other than the breath, say to yourself "craving" or "fantasy" and then gently return your focus to the breath. This will prove a great tool, both for bringing the mind back and for recognizing the distraction.

Part Two

bOW MEDITATION WORKS

Chapter Four

THE PSYCHOLOGY OF MEDITATION

To fully appreciate the practice of meditation, it is very helpful to understand exactly what we are doing and why we are doing it. As a child, I found it maddening that adults would tell me to do something without any explanation as to why. When pressed for a reason, I would frequently hear the well-known response, "Because I said so."

Unfortunately, many religious and spiritual traditions have taken the same attitude. They encourage a contemplative life involving prayer and meditation, but have done little to explain why it is so important. Therefore, in this chapter and the ones that follow, I would like to explore the 'why' of meditation. As we have already noted, meditation has some very noteworthy benefits, but the richness of the practice is greatly enhanced when the mechanics of the mind are more fully explored and understood.

I believe that meditation is a powerful and useful tool, and explaining how it works can only encourage its regular use in our day-to-day lives. So let us start with what I call the anatomy of the psyche. The psyche is the part of the mind that is conscious, though as we shall see, not all aspects of consciousness are necessarily part of our awareness. In fact much of the mind is very unaware of itself, which is one of the major reasons why meditation is so important.

As I write this, I am sitting in Golden Gate Park in San Francisco. It is a beautiful September day, and the lawn and gardens are lush and full. There are many tiny flowers in the grass around my blanket, and an attractive woman is jogging by. Not a bad moment. In fact, I would put it right up there on the list of great moments this week.

Everything I have just described is part of the first level of consciousness, which I call the 'Conscious Mind'. It is the part of the mind that is most familiar to us because that's where we spend most of our day. This is the level of consciousness where information about the world outside enters our psyche and is, for better or worse, judged.

Now the more weight we give to a certain judgment, the deeper that judgment sinks into the mind. We will talk more about judgments in a moment, but for now, let's just focus on the fact that we judge. Most experiences are judged, and it is the conscious level of the psyche that begins the process of filing those judgments in the nether regions of the unconscious.

And so the tiny sliver of the mind that is our conscious awareness seems to be all there is, but we know this is not the case. We dream at night and we make Freudian slips. We have episodes of déjà vu, and we make many life decisions without consciously knowing why. The unconscious mind is a vast territory, which for most of us is largely unexplored.

So let's take a look at the mind with its several levels and start to understand the anatomy of the psyche. I generally divide the mind into four basic parts. The lines between these levels of consciousness are blurry at times, but it can be helpful to think of them as distinct and separate parts.

Unified Field

The deepest level of an individual's mind is what I call the Unified Field (UF). This is a term I borrowed from Einstein. Basically, if you go deep enough into anything in the physical universe (including the human mind), you arrive at the same point. This point has been called many things over the years, but its nature is universally accepted to be an experience of joy and bliss. Some people call it the Promised Land. Others call it Samadhi or Nirvana. The followers of Jesus were instructed to seek the Kingdom of Heaven 'within' themselves.[1]

The important thing is not what we call this Unified Field, but rather where it is. The great mystics of the past would not have us look for it at the mall or even in a church pew. Rather, they would have us look deep within. This is meditation's ultimate goal.

---

1 Luke 17:21

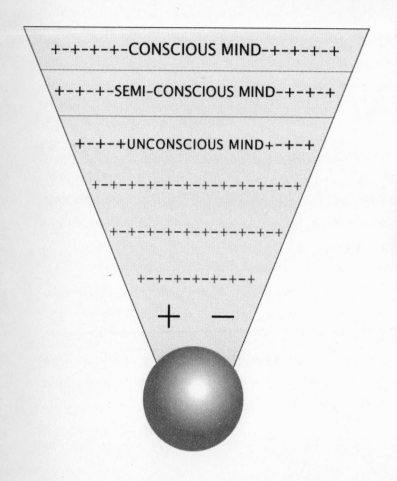

The Semi-conscious and Unconscious Mind

We have already spoken about the conscious mind. But what of the other parts? Let's start with the semi-conscious mind. This level of our consciousness is what we experience in daydreams and REM (Rapid Eye Movement) sleep. We can often recall some of our day-dreams and our dreams while we sleep, but at best they tend to be hazy and many details are missing.

That is because this level of the mind is only partially conscious. Our daydreams and our fantasies have an otherworldly quality that lives just below the surface of our conscious awareness. Even though we may have some control over these dream-like images, they tend to have a life of their own. There seems to be little choice in how we experience these images.

It is even harder to pin down the unconscious mind. While the images and dreams that we experience at the semi-conscious level are far-fetched at times, they at least resemble our daily lives. They are linear in nature and seem to follow most of the rules (albeit loosely) of the physical universe.

However, the unconscious mind follows its own set of rules. It is not linear and its content can often seem bizarre and illogical. Maybe it will be a fleeting image or a shape. Perhaps it will be a sound or a voice. These unconscious thoughts are sometimes beautiful and sometimes disturbing. One thing is certain however; we spend so little time there in a conscious way that this deep level of the mind is almost always strange to us.

Bending Spoons

So we have a mind with several parts: the conscious mind at the surface; the semi-conscious and unconscious minds below that; and finally our source point, the unified field.

When we spoke about the unified field, or source point, you learned that this is the part of the mind characterized by joy and bliss. These are two very desirable qualities, but we see them so rarely in the world. There is a very good reason for that. In spite of the fact that each of us has at our very core the qualities of joy and bliss, in between we have three levels of mind, filled with judgments.

If we didn't judge, that source would radiate joy and bliss through our mind to be easily expressed in the world. But most of us hold vast numbers of judgments that bend and warp our true nature into something that looks very different.

You see, every experience you have ever had – the big ones and the small ones too – has been judged by your ego. Some things are judged to be negative and others to be positive. In either case the ego places a little kink in the mind. Then, when the light of pure joy and bliss shines through it, it gets bent and distorted in the same way that a prism breaks light apart.

The goal of meditation is to remove these judgments so that more and more of our lives can be an expression of that joy and bliss. This, of course, can be a daunting task: removing all this mind clutter can feel a lot like cleaning out and organizing your teenage son or daughter's room.

Meditation's Effect on the Mind

So how do we do this? If the mind is filled with judgments and most of the mind is not even consciously available to us, then where do we begin? How do we begin to neutralize something we don't even know is there?

That is where meditation comes in. The whole practice of meditation is linked to raising awareness and neutralizing judgments along the way. As an example, let's look at my practice from this morning.

I started my practice the way many of us do – by sitting still and bringing my awareness to the breath. I had a busy day ahead of me, so I found myself drifting to thoughts of the day. There was an early morning meeting with a non-profit group about a fund-raiser, and I had to catch a flight to Washington, DC. My mind kept rehashing the day and trying to plan it out. I realized this a number of times and, each time, after acknowledging that I was in fantasy mode about my day, I returned to the breath. All these distractions were part of my conscious mind, and each time I decided to return my mind to the breath, these judgments lost some of their power over me.

Because I continued to return to the breath, the meditation technique took me a bit deeper and I reached the level of the semi-conscious mind. Here I found myself in a daydream about bumping into George W. Bush at a café while in DC and inviting him to attend the yoga workshop I was about to teach. After finishing the class, he decided to spend the rest of his term in office fighting for world peace, environmental stability and civil rights for all beings.

Now, as far-fetched as that daydream might seem, it was very fun to engage in it. I realized several times that I was being distracted and tried to return to the breath, but it took a good ten minutes before I could let the fantasy go. What was not quite so apparent was what lay behind this daydream. While it seemed harmless enough, behind it were the judgments held in my semi-conscious mind. They had created the whole thing. By constantly returning to the breath, I was able to withdraw some of the energy from them. This allowed me to move into the unconscious mind.

As I moved into the unconscious mind, I found myself distracted by a number of images that were anything but normal. First I saw my friend Christopher's head turn into a pumpkin with the standard jack-o-lantern eyes and mouth. Strangely, it still looked like him. Then he reached up and pulled the top off his pumpkin head and a white mouse holding a pumpkin seed scurried out and scampered off. I was quite amused at first, but quickly realized that I needed to return to my breath. Then I got distracted again. I started to wonder what that odd image meant. I labeled this distraction as a form of craving and moved back to my breath. I was starting to go into another image when I realized that it was time to end my meditation.

This morning, I did not get deep enough in my meditation to experience the UF, although I have visited it in the past. That was all right with me, though. It was enough that I had been able to let go of a number of judgments and return to the breath quite a few times. My mind was more still than when I had started and I felt ready to move forward into my busy day.

This is how meditation starts to reshape the way we think. We can use it to move beneath the surface of our minds and choose again. Most people spend their lives feeling like victims of luck or fate. This is because their most important decisions are made on an unconscious level.

By clearing the mind through meditation, we allow more of our decisions to be made consciously, which exponentially improves our personal lives and the quality of the communities of which we are a part.

Points of Interest

- All thought radiates from one central point. This source is known by many names, such as The Unified Field, God, The Great Spirit, The Tao, Allah and many others.

- The mind is divided into three basic levels:

    1. Conscious mind – experienced as conscious thought

    2. Semi-conscious mind – experienced as dreams and fantasy

    3. Unconscious mind – experienced as archetypes

- Our perception, and to a large extent the world we live in, are the product of our judgments. These judgments can be either positive or negative.

- An individual's collective judgments create an ego, which is the perception that the self is small, isolated, and finite.

Chapter Five

THE PHYSIOLOGY OF MEDITATION

In the West over the past few years, meditation has caught on like wild-fire, due in large part to its extraordinary physical benefits. Although the masters and teachers of meditation have long maintained that its physical benefits are a small fraction of the spiritual and psychological benefits, it is hard to ignore its healing effects on the body.

What was once seen as a weird activity reserved for hippies and mountaintop gurus is now becoming so popular that my HMO has a poster advertising a meditation class for people with heart disease. Opinion has come full circle, due quite largely to a number of studies printed in mainstream medical journals.

In addition, doctors such as Dean Ornish, Bernie Siegel and Deepak Chopra have sought to integrate meditation into Western medicine. Thanks to these pioneers, we no longer have to choose between Western medicine and Eastern meditation. The two are being more and more tightly integrated. The mind body connection is not only being acknowledged, it is being used to treat illnesses from AIDS to cancer to heart disease, with well-documented success.

Understanding the physiology of meditation is not essential. It will work for us whether we understand it or not. However, this understanding can help deepen our commitment to the practice and can also help us to work more consciously with the mind body connection.

Stress and Pressure

Before we can understand how meditation affects the body, we need to understand stress and pressure, because it is stress that causes negative responses in the body.

We all face challenges in life. Of course, some days or months or years are better than others, but life can be difficult. We deal with difficulties at work, in our relationships, within our families and with the deaths of people we love.

All these situations create what I call pressure. I call it pressure because it comes from outside of us. Pressure can come from many sources, but in all cases it creates a squeeze that can be difficult to process. Sometimes even the best events in our lives can put pressure on us. A wedding or a job promotion can be just as intense as the loss of a job or a divorce. Pressure happens when the world outside demands our attention.

Remember
> Stress is an internal response to external pressure.

This is an important distinction. While pressure comes from without, and we often have little control over it, stress is entirely an internal matter. Stress happens when the external situation becomes too overwhelming for the mind to process calmly, and we experience a change in our physiology as well as in our emotional and psychological selves.

We need to be able to distinguish the two because stress is often harmful to the body. We will cover more on that in a moment, but for now let's just focus on the difference between stress and pressure. Sometimes we can control the events in our lives and arrange its details so they produce less pressure. We feel less stress as a result.

Unfortunately this is not always the case. Oftentimes we have little say in what happens in life, and the pressure we experience can be overwhelming. This is why meditation is so important. Even though we can't control all the things that happen outside ourselves, through the practice of meditation we can control the stress response that happens within.

I had two friends, Michael and Jeff, who were lovers for over fifteen years. Jeff was diagnosed HIV+ about a year after they met and managed to live well for most of their relationship. He ate well, took his vitamins and practiced meditation. In fact, he didn't even take medication for most of the time they were together.

About two years before he died, Jeff started on an aggressive treatment recommended by his doctor. This was quite effective in lowering his viral load[1], but unfortunately it affected his cholesterol level and his heart, and he died of a fatal heart attack.

Jeff and Michael had been through a lot together and they used Jeff's HIV status as a springboard from which to jump high and celebrate life. Even though they had done a lot of spiritual work and had a lot of faith, Jeff's death hit Michael quite hard. He went into a deep depression and his life started to unravel. Everything from his job to

---

1 A test used by some doctors to measure HIV. A low or undetectable viral load is thought by many doctors to prevent or delay the onset of AIDS.

his friendships was deeply affected. Eventually he decided to take up yoga again.

After one of my classes we sat and chatted. It was amazing to see how much Jeff's death had affected him on a physical level. He was not just emotional. He had lost weight and his eyes looked tired. Even his hair looked unhealthy.

Michael was no stranger to meditation, and with a little coaxing he agreed to return to the daily practice that he and Jeff had shared each morning. It was about a month before I saw him again. What a difference! He looked much better and his eyes looked soft again. It was as if he had been drinking from the fountain of youth. I asked him how he was holding up, and he responded saying, "It is tough; I miss him so much. I still cry myself to sleep every night, and that ache in my chest doesn't feel like it will ever leave. He was my best friend. But the meditation really helps. I still feel the pain, but I am no longer crippled by it. It washes through me rather than knocking me over."

There is nothing Michael can do to change the source of his pain. He can't bring Jeff back and the grief of losing him is not likely to go away anytime soon. That event will continue to put pressure on Michael for many years to come. While the source of Michael's pressure is beyond anyone's control, how he responds to Jeff's death is another story. Because stress is entirely internal, Michael has a choice, albeit a difficult one. How his mind responds to that pressure will determine how much stress he will experience, and in turn how his body will be affected.

Stress and the Nervous System

As we mentioned, Michael's stress had a very noticeable effect on his body. This is true of all stress, for all of us. Stress in the mind creates a very measurable effect in the body, and usually one that is undesirable.

The body has an auto pilot system called the Autonomic Nervous System (ANS). The ANS is very important to our continued health and survival. It regulates many things that are beyond our conscious control, such as heart rate, breathing, digestion and immune function. These all happen in the background with little or no effort on the part of the conscious mind: You don't need to remember to beat your heart. It just beats. Further, if you decide to run around the block, your ANS will tell the heart to beat at a rate that is more appropriate for cardiovascular exercise.

The ANS also has two basic subdivisions. One is responsible for fight or flight[2], and the other for rest and digest[3]. Each of these has a very different but important function for our health and survival.

The fight or flight aspect of the ANS is responsible for getting us out of harm's way. It tells the heart to beat faster, the adrenal glands to produce adrenaline and the blood to flow to the limbs. For example, if you were walking down the street and someone jumped out of an alleyway to mug you, your body would kick into fight or flight mode.

---

2 Sympathetic Nervous System.
3 Parasympathetic Nervous System.

This would give you the biological resources to fight off your attacker, or run.

The rest and digest aspect of the nervous system is what manages the body's daily activities – things like digestion and elimination, immune response and our resting heart rate.

These two systems work well together for the most part. One gets us out of immediate danger and the other helps the body to nourish and heal itself. They work together to help ensure a long and healthy life.

However, the system has one flaw. The ANS can't tell the difference between a real physical threat (e.g., a person jumping out of a dark alley) and psychological stress (e.g., getting audited by the IRS). Both physical threats and psychological stress are treated in the same way, with some very unfortunate results.

Because the ANS can't tell the difference between a person jumping out of an alley and an IRS audit, it responds to both by tightening the muscles, constricting the internal organs and releasing adrenaline into the body. Together these responses put the important rest and digest functions on hold.

There are several reasons why this is a problem. First, we were not designed to stay in fight or flight mode for any length of time. Most dangers do not continue for years. While the fight or flight mode may be an important and lifesaving part of our wiring, it is not a place where you want to spend much of your life. Unfortunately, many people are so stressed that they spend almost all their time there.

Second, the fight or flight mode only helps with physical danger.

More adrenaline is not going to help with that tax audit or that difficult divorce. While those pressures may be the seeds of a lot of stress, they do not immediately threaten our safety. Addressing these situations from fight or flight mode is not only unhelpful, it can actually make it more difficult to resolve the issues.

Third, the long term effects of being in fight or flight mode are quite negative. Adrenaline may get you out of a tricky situation but it is very hard on the immune system. Constricting the organs may help protect them from attack, but it is not good to leave them that way for long: Digestion and elimination are impaired as well as the functioning of the kidneys and liver. Even the skeletal muscles will start to constrict, to be ready to fight or run. This is why many people get tight knots in their backs and shoulders.

Fourth and last, body and mind are very connected. If the body has posted a state of emergency, the mind has little choice but to follow. Remember, it is the stress in the mind that has created this physical state. It's ironic that the body's physical state will now worsen the psychological stress. It is a never-ending cycle that leads to more and more suffering.

Change Your Mind, Heal Your Body

All this talk about the nervous system is great, but it's just talk if we don't learn how to manage our stress. If people live under constant stress, their physical health will surely pay a price. It may start as chronic headache or heartburn, but eventually it can become something much more serious.

Meditation is a powerful medicine. The body is the servant of the mind. The body responds to virtually everything that the mind thinks. It doesn't matter what is real. If the mind thinks it, the body responds as if it were real.

When I was in high school, my mother woke me up in the middle of the night. She was visibly shaken and I knew immediately that something was wrong.

My younger brother Jason was sixteen at the time and had just received his driver's license. He was not in the house and my mother's car was missing. There was no note, and it was well beyond his curfew.

My mother was sure that my brother had been in a car accident or that some other awful fate had befallen him. One hour turned into two, and still he did not come home. My mother was sick with fear. Her body looked like it had been hit by an emotional wrecking ball.

Then, just as she was about to call the police, my brother came home. It turned out that one of his friends had just split up with his girlfriend, and my brother had gone over to his house to make sure he was okay. Because it was late, he hadn't bothered to wake my mother to tell her.

The truth was that my brother was fine, but my mother's head wove all sorts of stories about what might have happened to him. As a result of the activity in her head, her body reacted as if the stories in her mind were real.

Most of us do this all day long. Our minds create stress, and that stress triggers a physical reaction that most often is inappropriate. Rather than keep the body calm and relaxed, this stress sends the body into a downward spiral of dis-ease and discomfort.

We break that cycle when we meditate. We stop telling stories about what is happening and we allow the body and mind to find an appropriate response to outside pressures without creating a needless physiological response that does not solve the external problem and is actually harmful to our health.

The nice thing about the body is that it wants balance. If you walk into a hot room, the body will sweat to cool itself off. If you walk into a cold room, the body will shiver to create heat – all this to maintain a steady body temperature. The body wants to be balanced, i.e., in a state of homeostasis.

When we quiet the mind's stories through the practice of meditation, we allow the body to work its magic and find health. Until we quiet the mind, the body gets one mixed signal after another. Then health and balance become a goal that seems always just out of reach.

Practice Session

> Close your eyes and imagine you are in your kitchen. Notice its familiar sights and smells. Now see a cutting board and knife on the counter, with a large bowl of lemons on the side.
>
> Take one of the lemons and cut it into pieces. Feel the juice and smell the lemon as you pick up a wedge and bite into it. Feel the lemon juice fill your mouth and slide down your throat.
>
> Now open your eyes. Notice what has happened inside your mouth. Most people can create a physical change inside their mouths simply by thinking about eating a lemon. Just imagine how many things happen in your body all day long because of your conscious and unconscious thoughts.

Most of us who were raised in the United States have been taught that if you aren't busy doing 'stuff', then you are wasting your time. Then how can the practice of sitting in meditation be good for you? Let's take a look at the effects that meditation has on the physical body.

Cardiovascular and Respiratory systems

We place a lot of emphasis on cardiovascular health here in the West. Heart disease, high blood pressure and stroke are all among the top killers in developed nations. Most industrialized countries have done an adequate job of educating people about the dangers of a high fat diet and a sedentary life, but they have not done much to educate the public about the need to manage stress.

Of course, it is very important to eat well and exercise, but it can be a major support to add meditation to the regime. Meditation has been shown to lower blood pressure and improve circulation. Some also believe that the heart needs rest as well as exercise. Meditation seems to provide this.

The lungs are also affected by meditation. Researchers are finding that simply to breathe is not enough for good health. Quality breathing, which takes in the right amount of oxygen, is deep and full. Meditation helps us slip into a state where our lungs are working at their peak.

Digestion and Elimination

We have all heard of people who have digestive problems as a result of stress. Many cases of ulcers, constipation and diarrhea can be linked to stress. When the body is in fight or flight mode, the organs of digestion and elimination are hindered. They get less blood flow and are generally constricted. Meditation can help alleviate many problems in the gastrointestinal tract as well as in the liver, pancreas, kidneys and other organs that support digestion and elimination.

Immune System

Just now, the connection between meditation, the immune system and overall health is being studied in more detail. In fact, a whole new branch of medicine called psychoneuroimunology is evolving. This is very exciting news, because science is starting to catch on to what mystics have known for thousands of years. More and more, the effects of meditation on the immune system are being scientifically demonstrated and documented in medical journals.

The study of the mind body connection is a very new science, but the benefits of meditation and similar practices are becoming more and more clear. For its health promoting virtues alone, meditation is worth every ounce of effort, but as we shall see, that is only the beginning.

Chapter Six

MEDITATION AND EMOTIONS

During the month-long Yoga Teacher Training Program that I facilitate, we spend a lot of time in seated meditation. Every morning we have a two-hour practice, which includes an hour and half of yoga and a half-hour of meditation. About two weeks into this year's training a woman approached me. She seemed a bit distraught, so we went for a walk and found a nice seat overlooking a lush Costa Rican coffee field.

"I don't think I am cut out to be a yoga teacher," she said, tears filling her eyes. "I find myself crying almost every time I sit to meditate. I think there is something really wrong with me. I think I should leave now rather than waste any more of my time or yours."

I gave her a hug and reminded her to breathe. Once she had calmed down, I explained: "We are doing a lot of yoga and meditation. Part of this training is bringing you deep within and sometimes what you find there are some pent-up emotions that need to come out. Not only are you okay, you are clearing out a lot of stuff. All those tears are cleansing you and bringing you to a deeper understanding of yourself.

You are going to make a great yoga teacher, so hang in there."

In the beginning, most of us are quite shocked when emotions come up as a result of our meditation practice. A lot of us have the preconception that meditation will make us really peaceful and calm, and that sadness and anger will be a thing of the past once we start the practice. There is some truth to that in the sense that a regular practice usually leads to a more balanced emotional state, but you will probably need to work through a lot of suppressed emotions first. Working through them means feeling them, and that usually means shedding a few tears in the process.

If you develop a regular meditation practice, you can count on having an emotional release at some point. Of course some people carry more buried emotions, and others are more emotional by their very nature, but I have yet to meet someone who meditates regularly and who has not had at least an occasional emotional release as a result of their practice.

It is very important to learn to understand these emotions and how to deal with them. We live in a culture that tells us that emotions are a bad thing and that when we feel them, we need to control them. For men in particular, feeling emotions is frowned upon. Most of us tend to get uncomfortable when we see people cry because we think it means that something is wrong.

Actually, this is a backwards way of thinking. When we cry or laugh uncontrollably, we release intense waves of psychic energy. If this energy doesn't move, it builds pressure until there is no alternative but for it to come out in an inappropriate way. It is like damming a great river. The force of that river builds behind the dam. Eventually that energy needs to be released.

When we sit to meditate, we start to release, in a safe way, the emotional pressure that has built up within. The nice thing about doing this in the context of a meditation practice is that we have the opportunity to experience release in a way that is less destructive than your average nervous breakdown.

"Emotion – a mental state that arises spontaneously rather than through conscious effort and is often accompanied by physiological changes . . . ."
[—The American Heritage Dictionary]

Most emotions have several features or qualities in common. First, all emotions seem to be uncontrollable. In other words, they seem 'to just happen', perhaps because of an event, or a thought or memory. They may even occur as a result of a movie, book or piece of music. In any event, they seem to have a life of their own. They rise and fall like waves on the ocean: some big, others small, but there is little we can do to control them.

I once had a roommate who was dating this great guy who was good-looking, had a great job, and was fun to be around. Everyone liked him. Perhaps that is why everyone was so surprised when my roommate ended their relationship. When I asked her why she would let such a great catch slip away, she said, "Jimmy is a great guy, and I care about him a lot. I just don't love him. I want to, but the feelings are just not there. I can't make myself love him."

She was so right. You can't force emotions. You can't make yourself feel something you don't. How you feel is how you feel. Of course, as we shall see, emotions are very fluid and are in constant flux.

The second important quality about emotions is that you can't make them go away. They are there, like it or not. Of course we can deny them and pretend they don't exist. We can even suppress them and push them down into the nether regions of the unconscious. But eventually we need to deal with them in a healthy way.

Thirdly, there is a fluid quality to emotions, so that their nature is ever-changing. This is a very important aspect, especially when it comes to meditation. The fact that they are always changing means that if you sit with an emotion, it will eventually change. Where I grew up, there is an old saying: "If you don't like New England weather, just wait a minute, it will change." The same is true of emotions.

A fourth feature of emotions is that there are really only two, love and fear. Of course there seem to be many more. We can easily point to fits of anger and bouts of jealousy. We can remember times of great joy and contentment. But all the varied emotions we seem to feel have their root in only two. The first, love, originates in the part of our mind that is connected to Spirit. It is the source of all the different types of love, which include peace, joy, happiness and a whole bunch of other 'positive' emotions.

The other root emotion, fear, is always inspired by the thinking of the ego. It gives birth to anger, jealousy, rage, depression and all of the 'negative' emotions. If we were to trace our emotions back and really look at them, we would see that they can all be traced back to love or fear. Take, for example, if we feel jealous. If we really think about it, the emotion is not actually jealousy but the fear of losing someone we love.

Lastly, emotions never stop. You are experiencing emotions right at this minute. You have been having them every moment of your life. We just don't notice them all the time. The bigger emotions get more of our attention, but even in the absence of high drama, we are always emoting.

Practice Session
> Close your eyes and notice what you are feeling. It may be a subtle emotion, or it may be something grander. Maybe you are feeling happy or sad. Perhaps you are overwhelmed or relaxed. Just notice. Try this exercise again from time to time and notice how your emotions are always present and always changing.

When we consider emotions as they relate to meditation, we need to remember two important variables. Every emotion, whether based on fear or love, will have these two variables. Once we understand them, we can more easily endure the emotion they relate to.

The first variable is time. All emotions have a basic cycle, meaning they will last for a given amount of time. Granted, some emotions pass quickly while others may last for many years, but all emotions exist in time and are therefore temporary. This knowledge can be helpful, both on the meditation cushion and in life.

A while back I met someone very special. He was a wonderful human being and we made an instant connection. Like many new loves, it started out very intense and ended in a painful break-up. It was very hard to sit with the emotions of that break-up. There were times when I felt I would never feel the same, that I would never feel happiness and peace again. It took everything I had to keep reminding myself that emotions pass.

In time, that pain gave way to compassion and love. In fact it gave way to a love that was much deeper than anything I could have consciously planned. All emotions are like this. When we are in the middle of them they feel like the only reality we will ever know, and then they pass on to something else. The schedule is not ours to decide. Emotions run their course in spite of our wishes. There is nothing we can do to change that, except to prolong the pain.

Part of the problem, of course, is that we don't always like the emotions we are feeling. Therefore we want to make them go away, and so we use any number of techniques to suppress them. Some of us use food to numb out. Others choose sex or drugs. Even some of the new fashion pharmaceuticals like Prozac are very effective at sweeping our emotions under the rug.

All of these methods have an unfortunate consequence. None are able to shorten the overall amount of time we need to spend with an emotion. They simply act like a pause button. They seem to arrest the emotion, but they only delay the inevitable. Eventually, in this life or in the next, all those emotions will come out. When we learn to sit in meditation, we give those emotions the freedom to release healthily and safely.

The second variable that relates to emotions is their intensity. Not all emotions are created equally. Some emotions may be so subtle that they are barely felt, while others can be so intense they bring us to our knees. All emotions have energy behind them; the only question is how much.

I like to think of the intensity of emotions as being like the wind. Sometimes it is a gentle breeze. At other times it has hurricane force. It is always wind, but the varying intensities can be quite a dramatic experience. This is as true of 'positive' emotions as it is of 'negative' ones.

Most of us will have had the experience of being so swept up in love that we could barely move. Conversely, most of us will also have experienced occasions of loss or grief so overwhelming that we could do little more than lie down and cry. Whether the emotion is rooted in love or fear has no bearing on how intense it is. Yet, intensity is another thing we seek to avoid.

When emotions run high, our egos look to escape. Then, many of the tools to which we turn are the same as those we used to avoid the time variable: drugs, sex, food, shopping and any number of other methods are avoidance tools. Of course, this doesn't diffuse the energy that swells beneath the emotion, so we suppress it and all that energy builds up, just as it would in a pressure cooker.

You may be wondering what all this has to do with meditation, which is, after all, what this book is about. Meditation asks us to sit and stay present, regardless of what comes up. Since we are experiencing emotions all the time, and since these emotions can get intense, they can distract us from our meditation practice. When this happens we need to neutralize them in much the same way as we neutralized the thought patterns and memories that we encountered on the psychological level.

As if all this were not difficult enough, meditation also acts to deepen our awareness of the unconscious. It is in this unconscious level of the mind, as well as in the tissues of the body, that we store all that suppressed emotional energy. Therefore, to sit in meditation is not simply a matter of sitting and noticing the emotions of the moment, but it also opens the door for all the suppressed emotions of the past to reveal themselves.

So how do we handle this? If these suppressed emotions were too difficult for us to handle beforehand, why should now be any different? Why should we dig up the past?

These are all very good questions, and they have a simple answer. When we sit and meditate, we deal with emotions in a way that is decidedly different to the way that most of us have learned to handle them. Instead of trying to control an emotion, we learn to surrender into it. Seeing emotions like the wind is an apt metaphor. Like the wind, we have no control over what emotions arise. We have no control over how long they will last or even how intense they will be. However, emotions, like the wind, can be a very useful force in our lives and in our meditation practice too.

Just as we can use the wind to sail and travel great distances, so we can use our emotions to bring us to a deeper understanding of ourselves. Because our emotions have blown most of us around like feathers on the wind, we have learned not to trust their energy. However, through the practice of meditation we can learn to set our sails and let the energy of the emotions take us where we need to go.

How to Meditate when Emotions Arise

As we have said, emotions are bound to arise during your meditation practice. These emotions need to be addressed and not repressed again. In order to do this, we need to remember a few things. First, all emotions will pass. It may take a while – years even – but they will pass. Second, emotions can be very intense. Once we acknowledge this, we are ready to begin.

Let's use an example. Let's say you sit to meditate and the emotion of anger comes up. Sometimes you will have an identifiable target for your anger, such as a boss or coworker, but in this case let's say it is just a general sense of anger. Because the anger is rather strong, you may be tempted to psychoanalyze it. Or perhaps it is very intense and you want to avoid it by ending the meditation early, or thinking about something more pleasant.

Rather than give in to the above, choose to witness the emotion. Although your pattern may be to escape from the discomfort, this time choose to sit with the anger and continue returning to the breath. Remember that emotions are on their own timetable. Remind yourself that the emotions may not go away immediately, but they will surely diminish over time. With this awareness, you won't feel so overwhelmed by them.

Exercise
> The next time you are meditating and an emotion arises, don't push it away. Label it (fear, love, joy,

anger, etc.) and return to the breath. If the emotion continues to distract you, you may want to breathe rather more deeply to help keep your mind focused. It is important that you become an observer of the emotion rather than a judge. To let the ego judge and exploit you by creating a new story of its own would be like adding salt to a wound. Continue to acknowledge the emotion while always returning to the breath until the emotion passes, or until your meditation time is complete.

Finding Higher Ground

There are two benefits to working with emotions during a meditation practice. First, we have the opportunity to work through many of the emotions that have been hidden beneath the surface of our consciousness. This allows us to find more emotional balance in our lives and in our relationships, because we lessen the amount of emotional baggage we bring to every situation.

Second, meditation trains the mind to process emotions differently. Even though what we do on the meditation cushion benefits us greatly by freeing the mind from past emotional blocks, we would face an uphill battle if we allowed the emotions to come right back in. Luckily, meditation also teaches us how to process emotions in a healthy way. Thus they fill the mind less and less, and we find a greater sense of stability.

Third, the power that comes from sitting with emotions as they arise allows them to lift us to higher emotional ground. There is a lot of energy behind emotions, and the more intense they are, the more they challenge us. When we learn to ride the wave of energy that underlies all emotions, our threshold for handling emotions is raised. It is not that we feel fewer emotions. We feel the same number as before, but we aren't as easily crushed by them.

Once we find this higher ground we can begin to make decisions based on logic and inner wisdom rather than the ever-changing tides of our emotional bodies. This leads to a more balanced life and more satisfying relationships, and that is what meditation is all about.

Chapter Seven

THE GROUP MIND

Social activism is one topic that my new meditation students bring up all the time. In general, the people who are interested in self-improvement through the practice of meditation are also interested in improving their communities and the world as a whole.

Because of this, questions inevitably come up around the function of meditation in the healing of our world. It would seem, on the surface anyway, that meditation is nothing more than sitting around doing nothing when there are hungry children to feed and all sorts of other 'evils' to address. Let's face it, the world is not a very nice place for much of the time. Sitting around watching the breath can feel like denial rather than healing. Understandably, this is a cause for concern for many people.

There are many reasons why meditation can make the world a better place. In fact, in countries where meditation is practiced regularly, the rate of violent crime is significantly lower than in those countries that don't have meditation as part of their culture. The reason for this is multidimensional and understanding it can be a great help. Therefore, this chapter will focus on some of the basic ways in which an individual meditation practice can help heal our world.

Why is meditation good for the world?

- When you are more peaceful, you invite others to join in your peace.

- The only thing you can really change is your own mind, but that alone is enough.

- War is always based on talking louder, rather than becoming still and taking the time to listen.

- Meditation helps you to find happiness. What the world is missing right now is an abundance of genuinely happy people.

- The Unified Field is at the core of all living beings. The degree to which you and I connect with that field affects the whole world – like a ripple in the ocean of life.

The Productive Heart

On the most basic level, meditation enables us to be more focused in our work. We are all called to do different things in this world. I am called to write books, teach yoga and meditation, and do a variety of other things. Other people are called to be healers, teachers, soldiers, entrepreneurs, and any number of other vocations. These are part of our contribution to the world, but what we are called to do is not what is most significant. One profession or life's work is not more important than another. What is important is the energy we bring to our work.

When I travel to promote my books and teach, I often get comments about how productive I am. In addition to teaching in San Francisco I also go to teach in other cities. I am thirty-one and have traveled all over the world. I teach between six and ten yoga classes per week, and have written and published two very successful books. This is my third book, and the fourth is in the works.

I write this not to toot my own horn, but rather to demonstrate that meditation doesn't just make me a more peaceful person. It helps me become a more productive person. All of my success in life is, I believe, due to my spiritual practice, which includes seated meditation and yoga. We all have the potential to make our lives incredibly productive. We all have talents and gifts that are very much needed in this world, but distractions abound.

The practice of meditation helps us to organize our thoughts and structure our ideas. Through the practice of meditation, we can open up to the creative flow that is waiting to pour through us, infusing inspiration with passion. Meditation puts the mind in order and brings it under control, opening the door to receive this free flow of perfect energy.

The unfocused mind is like a sledgehammer, the focused mind like a sharp ax. Both tools can be used to take down a tree, but the ax is going to be much more efficient. Further, using the ax will allow you to work more swiftly, thereby expending much less energy and getting a lot more done.

With the mind sharp, we become more efficient, but it doesn't stop there. As the mind quiets, creativity increases. Our minds are in a natural state of creativity but that gets clouded by the business of our lives. By taking time to quiet the mind through meditation, we make way for wild creativity that offers a powerful medicine to the world.

I have two friends, Lance and Kathy. Both are exceptional people and are among the most open-hearted and compassionate persons I know. There are few in this world who are able to demonstrate such compassion and grace. In addition, each is an excellent writer with numerous good ideas for books they plan to write.

There is one key difference between them, however. Kathy has a daily meditation practice that she has made an important part of her life. Each morning she gets up, meditates for a half hour and then writes for an hour. Of course this requires she get up a little earlier than she used to, but the meditation seems to offset her need for that extra sleep.

Kathy is now publishing her second book. Lance, on the other hand, still talks and dreams about someday writing a book, but the busy chores of day-to-day life keep him far too distracted to write. As of now, his potential has not been actualized in spite of his open heart and good intentions. It isn't simply a loss for Lance; it is a loss for the world.

And so meditation gives us the two things we need most to make a difference in the world – a clear mind and a focused mind. Without these two qualities, even the most open and compassionate person will not have the discipline and structure to manifest that compassion in the world.

The Collective Mind

The benefits of an individual's meditation practice reach far beyond the individual and into the rest of the world. In order to understand the deeper healing that is possible, it is important to understand the collective mind.

Most of us think of the mind as being part of the brain. We also think that the mind is something that begins and ends within an individual's skull. This perception is understandable but unfortunate. Because we tend to understand things in physical terms, we also tend to think of the mind in terms of the primary vehicle through which it is expressed here in the physical realm, i.e., the brain.

The brain is not the mind. This is an important distinction. Mind is something much bigger, and on a very deep level all minds are connected. The mind is the 'soul', so to speak. It is expressed through the body, the intellect and the emotions, but it is none of these. The mind is eternal, infinite and unified.

This concept has most important consequences in regard to meditation. Because we are all part of one mind, the things I do with my mind have an effect on the collective mind that is shared by all of us. As difficult as this may be to fathom, we are all thinking with the same mind. It is only the ego that tells us we have separate minds. In truth, if you dive deep enough into any two minds, you will see that they meet.

I have often heard the collective mind referred to as the ocean. The ocean is one big body of water with many waves on top of it. The waves are connected to each other and the rest of the ocean, yet they seem to be separate. Our minds are much the same way. The collective mind is big and vast like the ocean, and our individual minds are like waves that rise and fall and then return to the ocean.

When we meditate we release old blocks and patterns that are not just our own. We collectively share all sorts of blocks and patterns known as paradigms. In order for a paradigm to shift into a healthier form, a majority of the individual minds involved need to change. This can be a slow process, but it does happen. Our history is filled with paradigm shifts that started off slowly and then, almost overnight, the tables were turned. Consider the following passage from my second book, *Yoga and the Path of the Urban Mystic*:

An example of this can be found in the story of the hundredth monkey, which is actually an illustration of human rather than animal behavior. As the story goes, a scientist was doing an experiment to see how fast a new behavior could be introduced into a tribe of monkeys. The monkeys under study lived on two islands in the south Pacific. Monkeys on both islands were given sweet potatoes to eat each day. These sweet potatoes were not native to the islands, so they were a new experience for the monkeys. According to most accounts, he took one monkey away from the others and taught it how to wash the sweet potatoes in the ocean before eating them. Then he released the monkey back onto one of the islands and watched to see how long it would take for all the monkeys to develop the new behavior. Gradually, one monkey at a time learned the behavior. It was a slow process at first, but when a certain number of monkeys learned this new behavior (one hundred is the number usually quoted), all the monkeys on the island began to wash their sweet potatoes before eating them. This rapid change in the community's behavior happened almost overnight.

The story gets even more amazing, however. At the same time that the scientist was observing the monkeys on the one island, he was also observing the monkeys on the second island nearby, using them as a control group. They were also given sweet potatoes, but none of them were taught any special behavior. When the hundredth monkey started washing his sweet potatoes on the first island, the monkeys on the second island spontaneously started washing theirs as well.

Subsequent studies have cast doubt on the accuracy of the story as told here.[1] However, its wide acceptance over the years suggests that it illustrates an important tenet of human behavior: our thoughts are available to all other members of our species, though they are free whether or not to think them.

Our history is full of examples of paradigm shifts. We know for certain that there was a time when most, if not all, humans believed the sun revolved around the earth. The idea seemed reasonable to the people of that time because of their limited perspective.

Then came Galileo, who had this crazy notion that it was just the opposite. People didn't like this idea very much. They were comfortable with their worldview and didn't appreciate people rocking the boat, so the church exiled him.

Of course, now everyone knows the earth travels around the sun. In fact, if someone were to tell you the opposite, you would consider that person ignorant at best, and probably crazy. Yet, not so many years ago Galileo was ridiculed for questioning that very idea.

---

1 For one such study, visit web page *www.context.org/ICLIB/IC09/Myers.htm*

We have seen these shifts over and over again throughout history. Movements like woman's suffrage, black civil rights, and the more recent battle for queer civil rights have all begun slowly, started by a few people who opened their minds to new possibilities. In time, when enough people had opened their minds, a nation-wide change happened. Not so long ago a woman couldn't vote and African Americans had to sit at the back of the bus. Now those things are intolerable.

When we sit to meditate we open our minds and clear away old ideas. In big ways as well as little ways, we are simultaneously clearing out the collective mind. When we do this, we become part of a subtle resonance that heals the whole of humanity.

I like to think of the collective mind as a big pie. Each of us is a piece of that pie. As we meditate, we start to erase those lines that seem to separate us so that we can begin to see the whole rather than the parts.

On a more personal level, our meditation practice will directly affect those around us. When I first started meditating and exploring other self-improvement techniques, my family thought I was going nuts. All of a sudden I was no longer playing by the rules that our family had long established. When I started to change my mind about life, my family had two choices. They could change with me or they could live in an awkward state of tension. For the most part, they have learned to grow with me, and in many cases they have inspired me to grow as well.

For example, my father and I get along quite well, but we are very different. Several years ago, I found myself in a relationship with a man. It was quite beautiful and I decided to share this with my family. I was

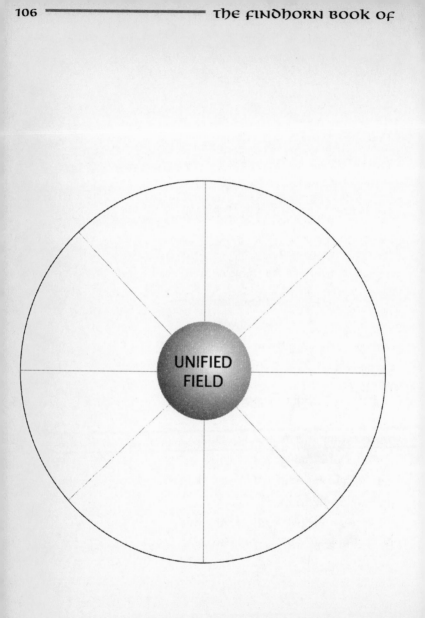

quite certain that my mother, brother and sister would handle it well, but I didn't know what to expect from my father.

My father is a great man who would never hurt anyone, but he is very 'old school' in his thinking. For him, sexuality and relationships have one primary function – procreation. So my telling him that I was in a gay relationship held the potential for disaster.

I spent a lot of time in deep meditation before I told him. I wanted to make sure I was grounded and centered for whatever his reaction would be. I wanted to be at peace, no matter what.

When I told him, he immediately went into lecture mode, "That's just not right!" he exclaimed. "It's just not natural. How are you going to have kids . . .?" He continued along those lines for some time. Then I interrupted him.

"Dad, I wasn't asking for your permission. I am in love, and I am happy. You are my father, and I thought you would like to know. I understand if you don't agree with my choices, but it is my life, and I have to do what makes me happy." I was not angry, and I was totally at peace. I truly didn't want to change him, and it must have come through.

"Well, it is your life. I just hope that whatever you choose for yourself, you will be happy. That's all any father can hope for his son." With that the subject was changed and we have not revisited it since. My father is still far from joining PFLAG[2], and he still seems uncomfortable when the subject comes up, but he was changed that day, and so was I. My meditation practice had a domino effect. Rather than take offense and fight and argue with my father, which would have been

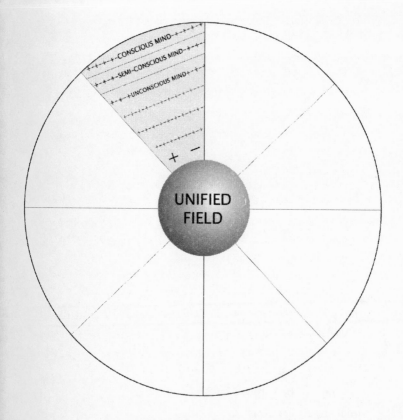

my previous reaction, I was at peace. This in turn invited him to be at peace, allowing the whole situation to unfold in a more evolved way.

Prayer and Meditation

Although this book is about meditation, I think it is important to mention prayer. While there is a subtle difference between the practice of prayer and the practice of meditation, they are closely related.

> Prayer is talking to God. Meditation is listening for his answer.
> [—*Alcoholics Anonymous*]

I believe that prayer and meditation are really one and the same at their pinnacle. Both lead to communion with Spirit and knowledge of our True Nature. Though prayer and meditation can look quite different, they actually complement each other.

The first stage of prayer is what I call desperation mode. This usually happens when we find out that we are in trouble. Perhaps the doctor has just diagnosed you with a serious illness or maybe your spouse has just asked you for a divorce. It is out of the desperation of life's situations that many people turn to prayer. This level of prayer usually sounds something like this, "Dear God, my life is a mess. If you fix this mess for me, I promise to be good . . . "

This, of course, is a good start. Even if it was desperation that

---

2 Parents and Friends of Gays and Lesbians (PFLAG) is an organization that many parents join to support their queer children. *(www.pflag.org)*

brought you to your knees, you are surrendering to something bigger and wiser than yourself. Unfortunately, if your prayer life ends when the crisis is over, another one is sure to follow. You can generally count on this cycle being repeated until you are ready for step two. Though, even at this point, a meditation practice can be useful because it helps us to slow down long enough to ask for help.

I think of step two as a major move toward responsibility because it is here that we stop expecting God to wipe up our spilled milk. Instead we ask for a paper towel so we can do it ourselves. A prayer at this level might sound something like " Dear God, I have made a mess of my life. Please show me how to clean up the mess I have created."

It is here that the practice of meditation comes in very handy. It is one thing to ask God for help in learning to clean up whatever mess we've made of our lives, but if we never quiet the mind and listen, how will we know what steps to take? Remember, it was the old thinking that created the mess. A new way of thinking is needed to get things back in order. Quieting the mind is the way we listen for guidance.

The third level of prayer has to do with day-to-day life. In the previous two stages we were praying because life had become uncomfortable. In this third stage we pray proactively. In other words, we turn our minds over to God before the milk even spills. This allows more and more of our life decisions to be made in conjunction with the rest of the universe.

Several weeks ago I was rock climbing with my friends Jasper and Nate. We were at Joshua Tree National Park in Southern California. The rocks we were on were a fairly easy climb so we were not using ropes or any other equipment. We easily made it to the top and enjoyed the breath-taking views.

The climb back down turned out to be more treacherous than we had expected. It was quite steep and virtually impossible to see where to put our hands and feet as we climbed down. For a while, it even felt as if we were going to need to signal for help. Then we decided to be each other's eyes.

As we climbed down, we relied on each other to know where to safely place our feet and hands. At one point, while Jasper was guiding me, I remember feeling a sense of trust. Jasper is one of my closest friends. It was nice to trust him with my life and to have no doubts that he was looking out for me.

Meditation helps us here as well. I needed to listen to Jasper each step of the way. Because of the stakes, my mind was very present to his words, but in the case of prayer, I am not always that present. The practice of meditation makes it much easier to learn to listen to the voice of Spirit guide you through life.

The last stage of prayer is really also the highest form of meditation. Each results in union of the small self with the True Self. Rather than having two wills (the ego and the True Self), we have only one will that is in perfect harmony with the rest of the universe. Rather than talking to God and making demands, the practice of prayer and meditation becomes like a perfectly harmonized song that brings with it perfect joy.

Group Meditation

Intention has everything to do with our experience in meditation. We have already noted the power of the group mind. The phenomenon of the group mind has been well documented, but usually in negative terms.

Take for instance the Holocaust. Hitler was able to convince an otherwise non-violent people that genocide was acceptable. Most Germans got swept up in the currents of false nationalism that resulted in one of the most embarrassing chapters in human history.

Most of us saw the same principle acted out in high school when classmates formed cliques, then dressed and acted alike. This kind of group energy has great power behind it and it can move people to focus their energy more deeply for good or for bad.

When we meditate in a group, we are tuning in to the same principle. We are agreeing to sit in stillness with others. It is a simple goal, but because it is shared with others, it can be a very powerful experience.

When I lived in Providence, Rhode Island, my friend Michael and I started a meditation group in our home. Our little group of seven people would meet every Sunday night. We meditated for thirty minutes and then discussed the experience. Even though I was meditating every morning with Michael, there was a noticeable difference in the depths that I was able to reach and how fast the time flew by.

Not only does meditation in a group help deepen one's practice, it also makes a common prayer or intention held by the group more potent. Prayers for people who are sick, or for peaceful resolutions to conflict, are much more effective when a group of people holds the same intention.

In San Francisco, a study conducted by Elizabeth Targ found that the effects of distant healing (various forms of prayer and meditation) notably improved the condition of the patients, who had brain tumors, heart disease or HIV. In the case of distant healing techniques directed to people with HIV, it was found that they were significantly less likely to develop an AIDS defining illness when they were being prayed for.[3]

Exercise

> Gather a group of friends together once a week. Meeting in a living room is fine. Agree to sit and meditate for thirty minutes. During the last five minutes of the meditation, hold a common intention for a person or cause you all feel strongly about. Try not to be attached to the outcome. Simply send your good intentions out and trust they will be received.

Meditation is a powerful personal tool, but the real miracle is how it helps to facilitate healing in the world. Sometimes this healing can be seen and measured, but at other times we have no idea how our personal practice is changing the world.

Whether or not we know the outcomes, meditation is key to healing our own personal sense of dis-ease as well as the conflicts that plague

---

3 *Health, Hope and HIV* by By Stacie Stukin (Yoga Journal)

humankind. It is for this reason that your taking time each day to still the mind is the greatest gift you can offer the world. The universe is a mighty garden. Your job is only to keep your little corner of the garden weeded. Meditation is the tool that allows us to do just that.

CONCLUSION

There was a time in my life when things seemed to happen to me without my having any control over them. Nothing seemed to run smoothly for me. My relationships, my work, school, and just about everything else I touched began to rot and decay.

For a while I blamed my parents, society, and even God. I was sure the universe was out to get me and that happiness would always remain an elusive carrot that would keep me running around the racetrack of life until I eventually grew weary. I pictured myself waiting to be put out to pasture so I could lie down and die.

Then something grand happened. I found the practice of meditation, and I began to live my life. I began to feel happy, and now fulfillment appears in almost every aspect of my day. It isn't that I never feel pain. Certainly I have had many difficult times since I began my practice, but those difficulties are less and less able to rob me of my peace of mind.

The other day I was speaking with my mother. Even though we had a rocky time through my teen years, we have grown very close and I consider her one of my best friends. Shortly after I started meditation my mother started as well. Once or twice a week we would go to yoga class or to Ellie's meditation group. It was a very special time because meditation was helpful for both of us, and we were growing together.

During this conversation, we were reminiscing about what a special time that was, and how much our lives had changed since. Since starting her meditation practice, my mother has gone back to college, divorced and remarried, started her own business and traveled around the country with her new husband.

More importantly, she is free.

"Darren, meditation has been such a gift," she told me. "I felt so stuck before. It wasn't that my life was awful. I just wasn't happy. There was so much I wanted to do, but could not seem to find the courage to move my feet. I knew I wasn't happy, but couldn't seem to find a way to make the changes."

"Once I started meditating," she continued, "things opened up for me. I started to think outside the lines, and all the energy I used to put into letting the neighbors think I was happy, went into actually finding happiness for myself. I don't know what the future holds for me. I don't know what decisions I will need to make tomorrow, but I do know this, I will never allow myself to feel trapped again. I now know that all I have to do is sit and be still. When I do that, all the pieces of my life come together."

My mother is such a wise woman. She has dedicated her life to her children, and I am so grateful that meditation has brought her the personal happiness that she has offered to so many others. The good news is that she and I are not alone. Anyone can find the peace that thousands of people around the world have found, simply by taking time each day to sit still, quiet the mind and listen.

When we do this, the rewards are countless and profound. From the physical benefits, such as reduced blood pressure and increased immunity, to the emotional benefits like a more balanced emotional state, meditation delivers its rewards quickly and without prejudice. You can be young or old, black or white, religious or atheist, cynical or naive. Meditation offers us an open mind and an open heart, and it helps us to heal ourselves and our world on every level.

Meditation is work, however, and to practice it consistently takes discipline and commitment. The ego mind will do everything it can to keep you busy, but in the end, all the ego's searching will only leave you feeling empty. In contrast, for all the hard work that meditation presents us, it also offers rewards that fill us from the inside by helping us to realize we are whole and complete to begin with.

And so I leave you with this thought. Look at all the things in your life. None of them mean anything without a quiet mind and a peaceful heart. Even our closest relationships will be strained if we come to them without first looking within. Therefore, make a commitment to seek peace within each day. It doesn't have to be hours. Twenty to thirty minutes will make all the difference. But give yourself and the world this stillness.

The time in my life when I felt like a victim has passed, thanks to meditation. I now make my own choices. They are not always wise choices, but at least they are mine, and if I don't like the outcome, I can choose again until I get it right. Through meditation everyone can take the wheel of his or her own life and choose peace.

May all beings be happy.

May all beings be at peace.

Om Shanti

Appendix A

FREQUENTLY ASKED QUESTIONS

How often should I meditate? How long should I meditate?

The nice thing about meditation is that you cannot meditate too much. I recommend a daily practice of twenty to thirty minutes. I would choose a consistent time each day and make it a regular part of your daily routine. The important thing is to be consistent with your practice.

How do I know when my time is up?

Knowing when it is time to end your meditation will get easier with practice. The more you meditate, the easier it will be for you to know how much time has passed. In the meantime you can take a watch and place it on the floor in front of you. Be sure to check the time when you start and make a mental note of when your time will be up. That will save you having to math when you check. Here are a few tips:

- Use a watch or clock that is easy to read.

- Do the math ahead of time.

- If you choose to use some sort of alarm, make sure it has a soothing sound.

- Don't end your meditation early. If you do, you will start a very bad habit.

- Remember to turn off the ringer on the telephone.

When is the best time to meditate?

There is no wrong time to meditate. There are, however, times that will be more difficult than others. Personally, I like to start my day with a meditation, but some find that meditating at other times of the day works better for them. The key is to find a time each day when you can sit. Here are a few other tips:

- Meditate at the same time each day.

- Avoid meditation just after a large meal.

- Use the ego's need for habit to your advantage to create a healthy pattern with your practice.

- Avoid meditation just before bedtime.

- Try making time to meditate twice a day.

Will meditation interfere with my religion?

The practice of meditation is not a religion. A religion is a belief system which some people believe in and others do not. Meditation is a practice that doesn't require belief in God or anything else. It can, however, be a great way to deepen one's religion.

Some religions oppose meditation. Usually this has more to do with fear and lack of understanding than religious conviction. If you feel that there is a conflict between your meditation practice and your religion, you may want to find a meditation technique that is rooted in your religious tradition.

Should I listen to music?

I don't listen to music when I meditate. Other people find it helpful. This is something you will need to explore for yourself. On the one hand, the music may be a noise distraction, but on the other hand, we live in a noisy world. The music may give you some sense of control over what kind of noise works best for you while you practice.

What happens when I miss a day?

Missing a day is not the end of the world. However, it is important that you are very careful not to let a pattern develop. Your strong intention should be to make meditation a daily practice. If you miss a day, don't beat yourself up. Rather, reaffirm your commitment to the practice and make sure you meditate as soon as possible.

Even if you miss a whole week or month, don't beat yourself up. Simply return to your practice and try to make sure you don't let yourself forget the importance of the practice. Just like you return to the breath, return to the practice because that is where growth happens.

My body hurts when I sit. What can I do about this?

In the West we are used to sitting in chairs. Sitting on the floor is not going to be easy at first, and accepting a certain amount of discomfort may be necessary. Here are a few other tips for making your body more comfortable in your practice.

- Invest in a good meditation cushion or pad. *(See Appendix C.)*

- Consider sitting in a straight-backed chair with your feet on the floor.

- Take hatha yoga classes regularly to help your body become more flexible.

- Stretch out your legs and hips before you sit to meditate.

- Use blankets to support your knees.

No matter how hard I try, I keep getting distracted. What's wrong with me?

Getting distracted is part of the practice. Your mind will wander. Count on it and expect it, BUT don't cater to it. If the mind gets distracted a thousand times during a sit, bring it back to the breath a thousand and one times. Meditation is not about avoiding distraction. It is about returning to the breath (or another point of focus) over and over again. It is the return from distraction that frees the mind and gives us control.

Appendix B

STYLES OF MEDITATION

meditation style	tradition	website
Vipassana (S.N. Goenka)	Buddhist	www.dhamma.org
Insight Meditation	Buddhist	www.dharma.org
Centering Prayer	Christian	www.centeringprayer.com
Jewish Meditation	Jewish	www.inner-meditation.org
Heart Rhythm Practice	Sufi/Islam	www.appliedmeditation.org
Transcendental Meditation	Yogic	www.tm.org
Siddha Meditation	Yogic	www.siddhayoga.org
Self-Realization Meditations	Yogic	www.yogananda-sfr.org
Meditation Center.com	General	www.meditationcenter.com
Darren's Cyber Ashram	General	www.darrenmain.com

Appendix C

MEDITATION PROPS
AND SUPPLIES

Yoga Props®

3055 23rd Street

San Francisco, CA 94110, USA

888-856-9642

www.yogaprops.net

DharmaCrafts: The Catalog of Meditation Supplies

405 Waltham St, Suite 234

Lexington, MA 02421, USA.

www.dharmacrafts.com

acknowledgements

Special thanks to my Family:

My mother Kathy Flynn-Ascare

My Father John Main

My Brother Jason Main and my sister Jennifer Main

Don, Josie, John, Sarah, Peter, Linda, Kate, Amy, Zoe, Tyler and Chase

Adalaina, Arthur and Mary, and all the Mains who are too numerous to mention.

Special thanks to those who have sat with me in stillness:

All of my students and teachers have been my greatest asset as I have walked the path of the Urban Mystic. Although I would like to acknowledge you all, my publisher wouldn't hear of it. There are a few folks who have touched my meditation practice so deeply that I wanted to mention them here.

Michael Lynch

Christopher Love

Jasper Trout

Jacki, Carlos, Kristi, Peter and Jimmy

Nicholas Lizza

Karin "Bhakti" Pratt

Tara and Tim Dale

Rusty Wells

An EXTRA special thanks to Ellie Brown for introducing me to the practice of meditation.

Special thanks to my Editors:

Sue Louiseau, Amy Khan, Gregory Johnson, and Ellen Shea. Thanks to all of you for your red ink and loving input.

Special thanks to Findhorn Press:

Especially Thierry and Karin Bogliolo, Tony Mitton and Anne Sullivan (at Lantern Books). It is an honor to be published by a press that offers the world some of the best titles in new thought, modern spirituality, and urban mysticism. Thanks for your continued faith in my work, and your tireless efforts on behalf of my books.

Yoga and the Path of the Urban Mystic

by Darren John Main

with a foreword by Stephen Cope

242 pages paperback

published by Findhorn Press

isbn 1-899171-39-8

Every day, thousands of people in the United States and other Western countries practice yoga in one of its many forms. People around the world are realizing yoga's amazing benefits and making it an essential part of their physical and mental health. However, these benefits are just the beginning of a full and rewarding yoga practice. Learning to use yoga in other areas of life can extend its profound benefits from the yoga mat to every aspect of the human experience.

Because the mystics from ancient India did not create yoga with our busy modern lives in mind, understanding this ancient practice can be challenging. In fact, yoga was originally developed for people who would renounce the world. Therefore learning to look at yoga in a new way is essential.

In *Yoga and the Path of the Urban Mystic*, Darren Main explores the time-tested practice and philosophy of yoga in a new way. By using modern examples from more than a decade of experience with this ancient practice, Darren brings the principles of yoga into clear focus and makes them user-friendly for yogis living in the modern world.

Spiritual Journeys along the Yellow Brick Road

by Darren John Main

144 pages paperback

published by Findhorn Press

isbn 1-899171-23-1

"*Spiritual Journeys along the Yellow Brick Road* is a beautiful and simple way of looking at life. It sheds new light on *The Wizard of Oz* and allows us to use this beloved story to explore the depth of our souls."

—Gerald G. Jampolsky, MD, Author of *Love Is Letting Go of Fear*

"Darren J. Main uses a timeless story as an oracle that reflects our human journey to the Emerald City of our potential. The author digs deeply into hidden meanings, and mines gems of insight sure to appeal to fans of Joseph Campbell, Carl Jung, and all of us who loved The Wizard of Oz."

—Dan Millman, Author of *Way of the Peaceful Warrior*, and *The Laws of Spirit*